THE BEAUTIES OF DR. ISAAC WATTS

The Beauties of Dr. Isaac Watts

Containing the most striking and admired passages in the works of that justly celebrated divine, philosopher, moralist, and poet: equally calculated for the communication of polite and useful knowledge, and the increase of wisdom and happiness to which is added the life of the author

BY THE

DR. ISAAC WATTS

CURIOSMITH
MINNEAPOLIS

Published by Curiosmith.
Minneapolis, Minnesota.
Internet: curiosmith.com.

Previously published as: Printed at Newburyport by EDMUND M. BLUNT for MATHEW CAREY, Philadelphia, 1797.

All Scripture quoted is from the *Holy Bible*, King James Version.

ISBN 9781946145284

CONTENTS

CONTENTS *(Continued)*

CONTENTS *(Continued)*

CONTENTS *(Continued)*

CONTENTS *(Continued)*

THE LIFE OF
DR. ISAAC WATTS

It is not to be expected that the life of a man devoted from a state of infancy to study and retirement, should be pregnant with such incidents as are apt to excite public curiosity. The truly excellent person of whom it is our business to present the reader with some biographical anecdotes, was distinguished by a cheerful and uninterrupted discharge of every religious and moral duty, an imagination so fertile in original and great ideas as to seem incapable of being exhausted, a profound and solid judgment, and very extensive literary acquirements.

Having premised thus much, we shall proceed to the narrative. The father of Dr. Watts kept a boarding school in the town of Southampton; and his qualifications for the office of a preceptor were such as procured him considerable encouragement, while the integrity of his manners gained him the respect of all who had the happiness of his acquaintance. Of nine children Isaac was the eldest. Though Mr. Watts was not in circumstances of opulence, yet his income was equal to the support of his numerous family in a style of gentility.

Isaac Watts was born at Southampton, on the 17TH of July, 1674. At a very early period of life he appeared to be strongly attached to reading; and this disposition was with pleasure observed, and carefully cultivated, by his parents. At four years old his father began to instruct him in Latin; and after having made some considerable progress in that language, and in other fundamental branches of learning, he was placed under the tuition of the Rev. Mr. Pinhorne, a clergyman of the established church, and master of the free-school at Southampton.

In this situation our young student afforded very early proofs of an insatiable thirst for learning, and of an uncommon brilliancy of genius, which indeed rendered him afterwards so highly distinguished in the literary world. His rapid progress in the learned languages, and in various branches of the sciences, together with the sprightliness and vivacity of his wit, which he had the happy talent of attempering with a degree of sober judgment, which was altogether extraordinary in one of his years, induced some liberal-minded persons to propose engaging in a subscription for the purpose of completing his education at one of the universities. This generous proposal, however, he declined with grateful acknowledgments, declaring his resolution of adhering to those principles he had imbibed from his parents, which impelled him to attach himself to the dissenting church.

In the year 1690, young Mr. Watts took up his residence at an academy in London, under the direction of the Rev. Mr. Thomas Rowe, who, it is recorded upon good authority, had not, during the years that he resided in his seminary of learning, a single occasion of addressing him in a style even of the mildest reprimand or reproof:—So early was his mind impressed with just sentiments of religion and morality, such perfect simplicity was there in his manners, and so indefatigably assiduous was he in his studies. His most intimate companions while at Mr. Rowe's academy were his fellow-students, Mr. Horte, afterwards archbishop of Tuam, and Mr. Hughes, the poet.

Mr. Watts became a poetical essayist at the age of fifteen, and this art he cultivated, though rather as an amusement or a relaxation from more severe studies, than as a matter of serious business, till he had arrived at fifty. For a considerable time before the expiration of his minority, he appears to have frequently directed his attention to Latin poetry, though not with a view of acquiring the reputation either of great learning or extraordinary talents, but chiefly to obtain a more perfect knowledge of the language. The strength of his mind, and his singular industry, are sufficiently manifest in these productions, which though probably the effect of no inconsiderable labor, and not to be placed in competition with many of his other pieces; yet there is so much propriety both in the sentiments and the language, and they so admirably correspond with each other, that commendation will even here be extorted from the utmost severity of critical examination.

In the year 1693, Mr. Watts joined in communion with the church of which his tutor, Mr. Rowe, was pastor. Having passed through a regular course of education at Mr. Rowe's academy, about his twentieth year he returned to his father's house at Southampton, where he was received with the utmost tenderness of parental affection, every opportunity being afforded for further qualifying him to assume that important station, to which in process of time he became one of the most distinguished ornaments.

Having resided two years with his father, constantly employed in ardent study, and in the devotional exercises of a truly pious Christian, he accepted an invitation from Sir John Hartopp to reside in that gentleman's family in quality of tutor to his son. In this situation he remained upwards of four years, during which period he peculiarly devoted his mind to theological and scriptural studies. His exemplary piety, the simplicity and easiness of his manners, his extensive knowledge, and various other great and agreeable qualities, established the foundation of that reciprocal and lasting friendship, which subsisted between this excellent preceptor and his amiable pupil.

On the 17TH of July, 1698, the day on which Mr. Watts attained his twenty-fourth year, he preached his probationary sermon at the chapel in Berry-street, London, to a very numerous congregation, who united in acknowledging, that, whether considered in a theological, a moral, or a philosophical point of view, the discourse of the youthful candidate for being admitted a laborer in the vineyard of his blessed Saviour Jesus Christ, would have reflected the highest honor upon a divine who had grown gray in the fatigues of study and the exercise of the pastoral functions. In the same year he was chosen assistant to Dr. Isaac Chauncy. But though his public labors procured him universal veneration, they were in a short time interrupted by a dangerous indisposition, which continued for the space of five months, and was supposed to have been occasioned by too rigid an attention to his studies, and the unremitting activity and fervent zeal with which he availed himself of every opportunity of proclaiming the gospel of Christ, notwithstanding the natural weakness of his constitution seemed but little adapted to such severe and constant exertions. But upon the reestablishment of his health, his pious endeavors for the salvation of the souls of his fellow-creatures suffered no abatement.

Mr. Watts was, in January, 1701, appointed to succeed Dr. Chauncy; and on the 18ᵀᴴ of March was solemnly ordained to the pastoral office; but presently after this promotion, he was attacked by a very painful and threatening illness; from which he recovered by very slow, and, for a long time, by almost imperceptible degrees; and indeed for several years after this shock, his health remained in a very precarious state. In the interim, however, that his congregation in particular, and mankind in general, might not be deprived of so invaluable a member of society, and so exemplary a minister of the gospel of Christ, by too strict an attention to the discharge of the duties of his holy office, it was deemed expedient that he should be relieved from too intense application by a regular and stated assistant; and accordingly Mr. Samuel Price was in June, 1703, chosen to that employment.

Being now afforded an opportunity of allowing his mind some relaxation from the fatigues of his pastoral office, his health was gradually restored; and he again returned to a diligent acquittal of his holy ministration; to which task, arduous as it was, he added that of establishing a society of the younger members of his church, for the purposes of prayer and religious conference; and to these pupils he, from time to time, delivered the substance of the book, which he afterwards published under the title of *A Guide to Prayer*.

Our divine continued in the regular attendance upon his public duty till the year 1712, when in the month of September he was seized with a violent fever, from which he was not relieved till the cruel disease had so shattered his nerves and enfeebled his constitution, that though he recovered the full powers and vigor of his mind, it seemed not in the least probable that his existence upon earth would be prolonged through half the number of years which he afterwards enjoyed. During this illness fervent prayers to the throne of God were frequently put forth in his own church, and also in many others, for the preservation of so valuable a life; and the ardor of devotion which was manifested on these occasions, afforded a very remarkable proof of the high veneration and esteem in which he was held by all ranks of pious Christians, and particularly by his brethren in the ministry.

Soon after being attacked by this illness, at his earnest entreaty, his assistant, Mr. Price, was appointed a pastor of the church jointly with him. Between these pious members of the Christian church there subsisted a friendship disinterested and cordially pious, till the death of Dr. Watts, who bequeathed a legacy to "his faithful friend and companion in the labors of the ministry, as only a small testimony of his great affection for him, on account of his services of love, during the many harmonious years of their fellowship in the work of the gospel."

The traces of his last indisposition were to manifest for the ease of his numerous friends, who severely regretted the very precarious and alarming state to which his constitution had been reduced; and among the most distinguished of these, was the late Sir Thomas Abney, who, with an ardency of persuasion which the sincerity and warmth of Mr. Watts' friendship for his generous supplicant, and a thorough conviction of his exemplary piety and numberless public and private virtues, disqualified him from resisting, invited our divine to establish his residence at his seat, at Stoke Newington.

While he remained in the family of Sir Thomas Abney, "the notions of patronage and dependence were overpowered by the perception of reciprocal benefits." About eight years after his removal to the house of Sir Thomas, at Stoke Newington, that gentleman died; and since a more pious and orthodox Christian, or a man of more exemplary virtue either in public or private life has been scarcely known, it will easily be believed that his death was sincerely lamented.[1] After the decease of his generous and truly respectable friend, he continued to reside in the family of Lady Abney till his death, including in the whole a period of thirty-six years, during which, both by that lady and her truly excellent daughter, the present Mrs. Elizabeth Abney, he was treated with the same uniformity of friendship which he had experienced during the life of Sir Thomas. During his residence in this happy family, which, as Dr. Gibbons justly observes, "for piety, order, harmony, and every virtue, was an house of God," his days ran on in an even tenor, diversified only by a succession of literary productions.

Without solicitation, or even a hint that the compliment would be acceptable, in the year 1728, the universities of Edinburgh and Aberdeen transmitted him a diploma, whereby Mr. Watts was constituted a doctor of divinity; and in this grant it must be allowed there was singular propriety, for he had long rendered himself worthy of the distinction, not only by his diligence and success as a Christian minister, but also by his numerous theological, philosophical, and metaphysical writings, and by being the man who had unquestionably contributed more than any other to convince the dissenters, who had been ever remarkable for an affected contempt of the beauties of language, and a studied inelegancy of expression, that the great truths of the Christian gospel would become doubly attractive

---

1 Sir Thomas Abney was several years an alderman of London; and he likewise served the office of Lord Mayor. As his private life was without reproach, so he discharged the duties of his public station with unimpeached integrity. He died February 6TH, 1721–2, in the 83RD year of his age.

when displayed in the fascinating powers of a polished diction.

In stature, Dr. Watts was but little above six feet. Though his figure seemed not calculated to command attention, yet in common discourse upon serious subjects, as well as in the pulpit, there was a dignified solemnity in his whole deportment and manner of utterance, that afforded a kind of irresistible energy to whatever came from his lips. Gesticulation in the pulpit he rejected, both as unnecessary and as little corresponding with the gravity and importance of divine topics: but in familiar conversation he was not so observant of a severity of manners; his fancy was excursive, and his wit was brilliant; and he sometimes exercised those faculties with freedom, though he ever restrained himself within the bounds of strict decorum, seldom dismissing a subject without deducing from it some excellent lesson of religion or morality.

While in the family of Sir Thomas Abney and his Lady, he constantly devoted one fifth[1] of his income to charitable uses; and he frequently visited the poor in sickness and cheered their drooping hearts with spiritual comfort.

Since his writings have been criticized by that eminent judge of literary merit, Dr. Samuel Johnson, it would perhaps be deemed a sort of presumption in the writer of this narrative, were he to obtrude upon the reader his own opinion as to the degree of approbation that is due to the voluminous works of Dr. Watts: and therefore he will introduce an extract, which, though concise, he trusts will prove satisfactory.

"Few men have left behind such purity of character, or such monuments of laborious piety. He has provided instruction for all ages, from those who are lisping their first lessons, to the enlightened readers of Malbranche and Locke; he has left neither corporeal nor spiritual nature unexamined; he has taught the art of reasoning, and the science of the stars.

"His character, therefore, must be formed from the multiplicity and diversity of his attainments, rather than from any single

---

1 Dr. Johnson says *one third:* but this I apprehend to be a mistake.

performance; for it would not be safe to claim for him the highest rank in any single denomination of literary dignity; yet perhaps there is nothing in which he would not have excelled, if he had not divided his powers to different pursuits.

"As a poet, had he been only a poet, he would probably have stood high among the authors with whom he is now associated. For his judgments were exact, and he noted beauties and faults with a nice discernment; his imagination, as the *Dacian Battle* proves, was vigorous and active, and the stores of knowledge were large, by which his imagination was supplied. His ear was well-tuned, and his diction was elegant and copious."

For between two and three years before his death, the activity and sprightliness of his mind suffered a gradual abatement: but in no other respect did his faculties seem impaired. Death had no terrors for a man whose life had been uniformly employed in preparing himself for the awful change which was to give him possession of those glorious rewards which he now enjoys through the mediation of his blessed Saviour.

Doctor Isaac Watts died at Stoke Newington on the 25TH of November, 1748, in the seventy-fifth year of his age.

THE BEAUTIES OF
DR. ISAAC WATTS

THE INVISIBLE NATURE OF GOD

We are the work of some more powerful and superior hand; but how we came first into being, we know not: the manner of our original existence is hid from us in darkness: we are neither conscious of our creation, nor of the Power which created us. He made us, but he hid himself from our eyes and ears, and all the searches of sense. He has sent us to dwell in this visible world, amidst an endless variety of images, figures, and colors, which force themselves upon our senses; but he forever disclaims all image, color, and figure himself. He has set us, who are inferior spirits, this task, in these regions of mortal flesh, to search and *feel after him, if haply we may find* the supreme, the infinite, and eternal Spirit. *We are* near akin to him, even his *own offspring;* but we see not our Father's face; nor can all the powers of our nature come at the knowledge of him that made us, but by the labors and inferences of our reason. We toil and work backward to find our Creator: from our present existence, we trace out his eternity; and through the chain of a thousand visible effects, we search out the first, the invisible, and almighty cause.

When we fancy we perceive something of him, it is at a distance, and in a dusky twilight. We espy some faint beams, some glimmerings of his glory breaking through the works of his hands; but he himself stands behind the veil, and does not show himself in open light to the sons and daughters of mortality. Happy creatures, if we could make our way so near him, as to behold the lovely and adorable beauties of his nature; if we could place our souls so directly under his kindest influences, as to feel ourselves adore him in the most profound humility, and love him with the most sublime affection. *Miscel. Thoughts.*

IDOLATRY

It has been an old temptation to mankind, almost ever since human nature was made, that we desire to find out something just like God. Hence arose a great part of the idolatry of ancient ages, and of almost all the heathen world. The Christian world, indeed, has much clearer light, and nobler discoveries of the invisible nature of God, and yet how has the Romish church fallen into gross idolatry in this respect, and with profane attempt they have painted all the *blessed Trinity!* Whatsoever pretence they may derive from the human nature of the Son of God, or from the dove-like appearance of the Holy Spirit, to draw the figures of a dove or a man, as a memorial of those sacred condescensions; yet I know no sufficient warrant they can have to fly in the very face of divine prohibition, and to paint and carve the figure of God the Father like an old man, when he never appeared among men in any bodily form; and our Lord Jesus himself says of him—*Ye have neither heard his voice at any time, nor seen his shape.*[1] *Miscel. Thoughts.*

THE STUDY OF MANKIND

Among all the useful and entertaining studies of philosophy, there is none so worthy of man as the science of human nature. There is none that furnishes us with more wonders of divine wisdom or gives higher occasion to adore divine goodness. *Miscel. Thoughts.*

ENQUIRY INTO THE SPIRITUAL AND ANIMAL EXISTENCE OF MAN

Now I stand, now I lie down; I rise again and walk; I eat, drink

---

1 John 5:37.

and sleep; my pulse beats, and I draw the breath of life; surely I have the parts and powers of an animal; I am a living body of flesh and blood—a wonderful engine, with many varieties of motion: But let me consider also what other actions I perform.

I think, I meditate, and contrive; I compare things, and judge of them; now I doubt, and then I believe; I will what I act, and sometimes I wish what I cannot act: I desire and hope for what I have not, as well as am conscience of what I have, and rejoice in it; I look backward, and survey ages past, and I look forward into what is to come. Surely I must be a spirit, a thinking power, a soul, something very distinct from this machine of matter, with all its shape and motions.

Mere *matter*, not into all possible motion, can never think, reason, and contrive; can never hope and wish as I do, and survey distant times, the past and future. What am I then? What strange kind of being is this, which is conscious of all these different agencies, both of matter and spirit? What sort of thing can I be, who seem to think and reason in my head, and feel and am conscious of pain and ease, not at my heart only, but at my toes and fingers too? I conclude, then, that I can be nothing else but a *compound creature*, made up of these two distinct beings, *spirit* and *matter;* or, as we usually express it, *soul* and *body*.

It is very plain also to me, upon a small inquiry, that this body and this soul did not make themselves, nor one another. I had no more hand in the union of these two principles, or in the composition of myself, than I had in the making of these two distinct beings of which I am compounded. It was God only, that great God who created both parts of me, the *animal* and the *mind*, who also joined them together in so strange an union. And if I were to enter into the mysteries of this union, it would open a wide and various scene of amazement at his unsearchable wisdom! *Miscel. Thoughts.*

THE PRAISE OF GOD

What is praise? It is a part of that divine worship which we owe to the power that made us; it is an acknowledgment of the perfections of God, ascribing all excellencies to him, and confessing all the works of nature and grace to proceed from him. Now, when we apply ourselves to this work, and dress up our notions of a God in magnificence of language; when we furnish them out with shining figures, and pronounce them with sounding words, we fancy ourselves to say great things, and are even charmed with our own forms of praise; but, alas! the highest and best of them, set in a true light, are but the feeble voice of a creature, spreading before the almighty being that made him, some of his own low and little ideas, and telling him what he thinks of the great God, and what God has done. When the holy psalmist would express his honorable thoughts of his Maker, they amount only to this, *Thou art good, and thou doest good.*[1] How inconsiderable an offering is this for a God! and yet how condescending is his love, that he looks down, and is well pleased to receive it. *Miscel. Thoughts.*

SPRING

What astonishing variety of artifices, what innumerable millions of exquisite works is the God of nature engaged in every moment! How gloriously are his all-pervading wisdom and power employed in this useful season of the year, this spring of nature! What infinite myriads of vegetable beings is he forming this very moment, in their roots and branches, in their leaves and blossoms, their seeds and fruit! Some, indeed, began to discover their bloom amidst the snows of January, or under the rough cold blasts of March: those flowers are withered and vanished in April, and their seeds are now ripening to perfection. Others are showing themselves this day in all their blooming pride and beauty; and while they adorn the gardens and meadows with gay and glowing colors, they promise their fruits in the day of harvest. The whole nation of vegetables is under the divine care and culture; his hand forms them, day and night, with admirable skill and unceasing operation, according to

---

1 Psalm 119:68.

the natures he first gave them, and produces their buds and foliage, their flowery blossoms, and rich fruits, in their appointed months. Their progress in life is exceeding swift at this season of the year; and their successive appearances, and sweet changes of raiment, are visible almost hourly.

But these creatures are of lower life, and give but feebler displays of the Maker's wisdom. Let us raise our contemplations another story, and survey a nobler theatre of divine wonders. What endless armies of animals is the hand of God molding and figuring this very moment through out his brutal dominions! What immense flights of little birds are now fermenting in the egg, heaving and growing towards shape and life! What vast flocks of four-footed creatures, what droves of large cattle are now framed in their early embryos, imprisoned in the dark cells of nature! And others, perhaps, are moving towards liberty, and just preparing to see the light. What unknown myriads of insects, in their various cradles and nesting-places, are now working towards vitality and motion! And thousands of them with their painted wings just beginning to unfurl, and expand themselves into fluttering and daylight, while other families of them have forsaken their husky beds, and exult and glitter in the warm sunbeams!

An exquisite world of wonders is complicated even in the body of every little insect, an ant, a gnat, a mite, that is scarce visible to the naked eye. Admirable engines! which a whole academy of philosophers could never contrive; which the nations of poets has neither art nor colors to describe, nor has a world of mechanics skill enough to frame the plainest or coarsest of them. Their nerves, their muscles, and the minute atoms which compose the fluids fit to run in the little channels of their veins, escape the notice of the most sagacious mathematician, with all his aid of glasses. The active powers and curiosity of human nature are limited in their pursuit, and must be content to lie down in ignorance.

It is a sublime and constant triumph over all the intellectual powers of man, which the great God maintains every moment in these inimitable works of nature, in these impenetrable recesses and mysteries of divine art! The flags and banners of almighty wisdom are now displayed round half the globe, and the other half waits the return of the sun to spread the same triumph over the southern world. The very sun in the firmament is God's prime minister in this wondrous world of beings, and he works with sovereign vigor on the surface of the earth, and spreads his influence deep under the clods to every root and fiber, molding them into their proper forms by divine direction. There is not a plant, nor a leaf, nor one little branching thread, above or beneath the ground, that escapes the eye or influence of this benevolent star; an illustrious emblem of the omnipotence and universal activity of the Creator. *Miscel. Thoughts.*

DIRECTIONS CONCERNING OUR IDEAS

Furnish yourselves with a rich variety of ideas; acquaint yourselves with things ancient and modern; things natural, civil, and religious; things domestic and national; things of your native land, and of foreign countries; things present, past, and future; and, above all, be well acquainted with your God and yourselves; learn animal nature, and the workings of your own spirits. Such a general acquaintance with things will be of very great advantage. *Logic.*

SUPERFICIAL OBSERVERS

There are some persons who never arrive at any deep, solid, or valuable knowledge, in any science, or any business of life, because they are perpetually fluttering over the surface of things, in a curious or wandering search of infinite variety, ever hearing, reading, or asking after something new, but impatient of any labor to lay up and preserve the ideas they have gained: their souls may be compared to a looking glass, that wheresoever you turn it it receives the images of all objects, but retains none. *Logic.*

READING

If the books which you read are your own, mark with a pen, or a pencil, the most considerable things in them, which you desire to remember. Thus you may read that book the second time over with half the trouble, by your eye running over the paragraphs which your pencil has noted. It is but a very weak objection against this practice, to say, *I shall spoil my book;* for I persuade myself, that you did not buy it as a bookseller, to sell it again for gain, but as a scholar, to improve your mind by it; and if the mind be improved, your advantage is abundant, though your book yields less money to your executors. This advice of writing, marking, and reviewing your remarks, refers chiefly to those occasional notions you meet with either in reading or in conversation; but when you are directly or professedly pursuing any subject of knowledge in a good system, in your younger years, the system itself is your common-place book, and must be entirely reviewed. The same may be said concerning any treatise which closely, succinctly, and accurately handles any particular theme. *Logic.*

THE BOUNTY OF THE CREATOR

What is more necessary for the support of life than food? Behold, the earth is covered with it all around; grass, herbs, and fruit, for beasts and men, were ordained to overspread all the surface of the ground, so that an animal could scarce wander any where, but his food was near him. Amazing provision for such an immense family! What are the sweetest colors in nature, the most delightful to the eye, and the most refreshing too? Surely the green and blue claim this preeminence. Common experience, as well as philosophy, tells us, that bodies of green and blue colors send us such rays of light to our eyes, as are least hurtful or offensive; we can endure them longest, whereas the red and yellow, or orange color, send more uneasy rays in abundance, and give greater confusion and pain to the eye; they dazzle it sooner, and tire it quickly with a little intent gazing; therefore the divine goodness dressed all the heavens in blue, and the earth in green. Our habitation is overhung with a canopy of most beautiful azure, and a rich verdant pavement is spread under our feet, that the eye may be pleased and easy wheresoever it turns itself, and that the most universal objects it has to converse with might not impair the spirits, and make the sense weary.

I.

When God the new-made world survey'd,
  His word pronounc'd the building good;
Sun-beams and light the heavens array'd,
  And the whole earth was crown'd with food.

II.

Colors that charm and please the eye,
  His pencil spread all nature round;
With pleasing blue he arch'd the sky,
  And a green carpet dress'd the ground.

III.

Let envious atheists ne'er complain
  That nature wants, or skill, or care;
But turn their eyes all round in vain,
  T' avoid their Maker's goodness there.

Miscel. Thoughts.

WONDER

When we perceive any object that is rare and uncommon, that is new and strange, either for its kinds, or for its qualities; or when we meet with such an occurrence or event as is unusual or unexpected; or such as is, at least, unusual at such a particular time and place, we are struck with admiration or wonder, and that without any consideration whether the object be valuable or worthless, whether it be good or evil. We wonder at a very great or a very little man, a dwarf, or a giant; at a very little horse, at a huge snake or toad, at an elephant, or a whale, or a comet, or at any large performances of art, as moving machines, such as clocks, watches, with a variety of uncommon motions and operations: we wonder at a piece of extraordinary wit, skill, or learning, even at artificial trifles, as a flea kept alive in a chain; at any uncommon appearances in nature discovered by a telescope, a microscope, etc. Admiration has no regard to the agreeableness or disagreeableness of the object, but only to the rarity of it. And for this reason wonder seems to be the first of the passions. *Doctrine of the Passions.*

Let it be observed, that this passion has properly no opposite; because, if the object be not rare or new, or if the appearances be not sudden or unexpected, but a mere common or familiar thing, or an expected occurrence, we receive it with great calmness, and feel no such commotion of nature about it; we treat it with neglect instead of wonder. Now neglect is no passion. The rest of the passions, at least the most of them, go in pairs. *Doctrine of the Passions.*

BENEVOLENCE AND COMPLACENCE

Benevolence is sometimes laid out upon an object that has no such present good in it as we can desire or delight in, but only some foundation of future good, or some capacity to be made good or agreeable. A pious man can never love wicked men with the love of complacency or delight, but he may exercise the love of benevolence towards them, to pity them, and to wish their recovery. So our Saviour could not love the bloody city of Jerusalem with complacency, because it killed the prophets, and blasphemed God and his Son; but he loved it with benevolence, and wept over it some tears of compassion. *Doctrine of the Passions.*

PASSIONS INFLUENCED BY DIFFERENT SITUATIONS IN LIFE

Different employments, and different conditions of life, beget in us a tendency to our different passions. Those who are exalted above others in their daily stations, and especially if they have to do with many persons under them, and in many affairs, are too often tempted to the haughty, the morose, the surly, and the more unfriendly ruffles and disturbances of nature, unless they watch against them with daily care. The commanders in armies and navies, the governors of work-houses, the masters of public schools, or those who have a great number of servants under them, and a multitude of cares and concerns in human life, should continually set a guard upon themselves, lest they get a habit of affected superiority, pride, and vanity of mind, of fretfulness, impatience, and criminal anger. *Doctrine of the Passions.*

TO SUBDUE PRIDE

Consider what you shall be. Your flesh returns to corruption and common earth again; nor shall your dust be distinguished from the meanest beggar or slave; no, nor from the dust of brutes and insects, or the most contemptible of creatures. And as for your soul, that must stand before God, in the world of spirits, on a level with the rest of mankind, and divested of all your haughty and flattering circumstances. None of your vain distinctions in this life shall attend you to the judgment-seat. Keep this tribunal in view, and pride will wither, and hang down its head. *Doctrine of the Passions.*

GRACE AT MEALS

The conversation turned upon the subject of saying grace before and after meat. When several of the company had given their thoughts, *Serenus* acknowledged it was not necessary to offer a solemn and particular petition to heaven on the occasion of every bit of bread that we tasted, or when we drink a glass of wine with a friend; nor was it expected we should make a social prayer when persons, each for themselves, took a slight repast in a running manner; either the general morning devotion is supposed sufficient to recommend such transient actions and occurrences to the divine blessing, or a sudden secret wish, sent up to heaven in silence, might answer such a purpose in the Christian life; but when a whole family sits down together to make a regular and stated meal, it was his opinion, that the great God should be solemnly acknowledged as the giver of all the good things we enjoy; and the practice of our Saviour and St. Paul has set us an illustrious example. *Miscel. Thoughts.*

THE CHURCH-YARD

What a multitude of beings, noble creatures, are here reduced to dust! God has broken his own best workmanship to pieces, and demolished, by thousands, the finest earthly structures of his own building. Death has entered in, and reigned over this town for many successive centuries; it had its commission from God, and it has devoured multitudes of men! *Miscel. Thoughts.*

Go to the church-yard, then, O sinful and thoughtless mortal; go learn from every tombstone, and every rising hillock, that *the wages of sin is death.*[1] Learn, in silence, among the dead, that lesson which infinitely concerns all the living; nor let thy heart be ever at rest, till thou art acquainted with Jesus, *who is the resurrection and the life.*[2] *Miscel. Thoughts.*

A THOUGHT ON DEATH

Death, to a good man, is but passing through a dark entry, out of one little dusky room of his father's house into another that is fair and large, lightsome and glorious, and divinely entertaining. O may the rays and splendor of my heavenly apartment shoot far downward, and gild the dark entry with such a cheerful gleam, as to banish every fear when I shall be called to pass through. *Miscel. Thoughts.*

HUMAN EXCELLENCIES AND DEFECTS

There is nothing on earth excellent on all sides; there must be something wanting in the best of creatures, to show how far they are from perfection. God has wisely ordained it, that excellencies and defects should be mingled among men; advantage and disadvantage are thrown into the balance; the one is set over against the other, that no man might be supremely exalted, and none utterly contemptible. *Miscel. Thoughts.*

SELF-LOVE

Youth is wild and licentious. In those years we persuade ourselves

---

1 Romans 6:23.
2 John 11:25.

that we are only making a just use of liberty. In that scene of folly we are light and vain, and set no bounds to the frolic humor; yet we fancy it is merely an innocent gaiety of heart, which belongs to the springs of nature, and the blooming hours of life. In the age of manhood, a rugged or a haughty temper is angry or quarrelsome; the fretful and the peevish in elder years, if not before, are ever kindling into passion and resentment; but they all agree to pronounce their furious or fretful conduct a mere necessary reproof of the indignities which were offered them by the world. Self-love is fruitful of fine names for its own iniquities. Others are sordid and covetous to a shameful degree, uncompassionate and cruel to the miserable; and yet they take this vile practice to be only a just exercise of frugality, and a dutiful care of their own household. Thus every vice that belongs to us is construed into a virtue; and if there are any shadows or appearances of virtue upon us, these poor appearances and shadows are magnified and realized into the divine qualities of an angel. We, who pass these just censures on the follies of our acquaintance, perhaps approve the very same things in ourselves, by the influence of the same native principle of flattery and self-fondness. *Miscel. Thoughts.*

TRUST IN THE SON OF GOD

They that have trusted in the Son of God, begin to find peace in their own consciences; they can hope God is reconciled to them through the blood of Christ, that their iniquities are atoned for, and that peace is made betwixt God and them. This belongs only to the doctrine of Christ, and witnesses it to be divine; for there is no religion that ever pretended to lay such a foundation of pardon and peace, as the religion of the Son of God does; for he has made himself a propitiation; Jesus the righteous is become our reconciler, by becoming a sacrifice. "Him that God set forth for a propitiation, through faith in his blood, to declare his righteousness for the remission of sins that are past; that he might be just, and the justifier of him that believes in Jesus."[1] Therefore, being justified by

---

1 Romans 3:25, 26.

faith, we have peace with God.[1] Behold the Lamb of God, that takes away the sins of the world![2] was the language of John, who was the forerunner of our religion, and took a prospect of it at a little distance: and much more of the particular glories and blessings of this atonement is displayed by the blessed apostles, the followers of the Lamb. Other religions, that have been drawn from the remains of the light of nature, or that have been invented by the superstitious fears and fancies of men, and obtruded on mankind by the craft of their fellow creatures, are at a loss in this instance, and cannot speak solid peace and pardon. *Sermons, vol. 1.*

CONTEMPT OF THE TRIFLES OF THIS WORLD

If we look upward to heaven, we shall behold there all the inhabitants looking down with a sacred contempt upon the trifles, amusements, businesses, and cares of this present life, that engross our affections, awaken our desires, fill our hearts with pleasure or pain, and our flesh with constant labor. With what holy scorn do you think those souls, who are dismissed from flesh, look down upon the hurries and bustles of the present state in which we are engaged? They dwell in the full sight of those glories which they hope for here on earth, and their intimate acquaintance with the pleasures of that upper world, and the divine sensations that are raised in them there, make them contemn all the pleasures of this state, and every thing below heaven. This is a part of eternal life; this belongs, in some degree, to every believer; for he is not a believer that is not got above this world in a good measure; he is not a Christian, who is not weaned, in some degree, from this world: For this is our victory, whereby we overcome the world, even our faith. He that is born of God, overcomes the world;[3] he that believes in Jesus, is born of God. Whence the argument is plain, he that believes in Jesus, the Son of God, overcomes this present world. And where Christianity

---

1 Romans 5:1.
2 John 1:29.
3 1 John 5:4.

is raised to a good degree of life and power in the soul, where we see the Christian got near to heaven, he is, as it were, a fellow for angels, a fit companion for the *spirits of the just made perfect*.[1] The affairs of this life are beneath his best desires and his hopes; he engages his hand in them so far as God his Father appoints his duty; but he longs for the upper world, where his hopes are gone before: "When shall I be entirely dismissed from this labor and toil? The gaudy pleasures this world entertains me with, are no entertainments to me; I am weaned from them, I am born for above." This is the language of that faith that overcomes the world; and faith, where it is wrought in truth in the soul, has, in some measure, this effect; and where it shines in its brightness, it has, in a great degree, this sublime grace accompanying it; or rather (shall I say?) this peace of heavenly glory. Pain and sickness, poverty and reproach, sorrow and death itself, have been contemned by those that have believed in Christ Jesus, with much more honor to Christianity than ever was brought to other religions. *Sermons, vol.* 1.

INIMITABLE PERFECTION OF THE GOSPEL

The gospel of Christ is like a seal or signet, of such divine graving, that no created power can counterfeit it; and when the Spirit of God has stamped this gospel on the soul, there are so many holy and happy lines drawn or impressed thereby, so many sacred signatures and divine features stamped on the mind, that give certain evidence both of a heavenly signet and a heavenly operator. *Sermons, vol.* 1.

PROSPECT OF DEATH

"How should we rejoice in hope of that hour that shall release us from the sinful flesh, and when we shall serve God in spirit without a clog, without a tempter!" O, with what a relish of sacred pleasure should a saint read those words in 2 Corinthians 5:8. "Absent from the body, and present with the Lord?" Absent from this traitor, this vexing enemy, that we constantly carry about with us! Absent from the clog and chain of this sinful flesh, the prison wherein we are

1 Hebrews 12:23.

kept in constant darkness, and are confined from God! Absent from these eyes, that have drawn our souls afar from God by various temptations! And absent from these ears, by which we have been allured to transgression and defiling iniquities! Absent from these lusts and passions, from that fear and that hope, that pleasure and that pain, that love, that desire, and anger, which are all carnal, and seated in the fleshy nature, and become the spring and occasion of so much sin and mischief to our souls in this state. *Absent from the body, and present with the Lord.* I think there is a heaven contained in the first part of those words, *absent from the body;* and a double happiness in the last, *present with the Lord:* present with him who has saved our spirits through all the days of our Christian conflict, and has given us the final victory: present with that God who shall eternally influence us to all holiness, who shall for ever shine upon us with his own beams, and make us conformable to his own holy image: present with that Lord and Saviour, from whom it shall not be in the power of all creatures to divert or draw us aside. *Sermons, vol.* 1.

SUBSTANCE OF NATURAL RELIGION

Doubtless man must know and believe in the first place, that there is a God, and that this God *is but One;* for God is too jealous of his honor and dignity, and too much concerned in this important point, to lavish out happiness, and his heavenly favors, on any person who makes other gods to become his rivals; or who exalts a creature, or a more chimera, into the throne of God. He must believe, also, that God is a being of perfect wisdom, power, and goodness, and that he is the righteous governor of the world.

Man must also know, that he himself is a creature of God, furnished with a faculty of understanding to perceive the general difference between good and evil, in the most important instances of it; and endowed with a will, which is a power to choose or to refuse the evil or the good; that he is obliged to exert these powers or faculties in a right manner, both towards God and towards himself, as well as his neighbor. I do not insist upon it, that he must know these propositions explicitly, and in a philosophical manner; but he must have some sort of consciousness of his own natural powers, to know and distinguish, to choose or to refuse good or evil, and must be sensible of his obligations to inquire and practice what is good, and to avoid what is evil.

As for the duties that relate to God, man is obliged to worship him with reverence, to honor him in his heart and life, on account of his wisdom and power manifested in the world; to fear his majesty, to love him, and hope in his goodness, to give him thanks for what instances of it he partakes of, to seek to him for what blessings he wants, and to carry it toward him as his Maker, his Lord, and his Governor.

He must know also, that since God is a "righteous governor," if he does not make good men happy in this world, and the wicked miserable, then there must be another world, wherein he will appoint some happiness for the good, and misery for the wicked; or, in general, that he will, some time or other, distribute rewards and punishments to all persons according to their behavior: for this has a very considerable influence into all holiness of life, and every part of morality, which will hardly be practiced without these motives.

As for the duties which relate to other men, every man must know and believe, that he is placed here among a multitude of fellow creatures of his own species or kind, he is bound to practice truth or veracity, justice and goodness, toward them, according to the several relations in which they may stand, as a father, brother, son, husband, neighbor, subject, master, servant, buyer, seller, etc.

And with regard to himself, he is bound to exercise sobriety and temperance, and to maintain a due government over his appetites and passions, that they run not into excess and extravagance.

And, finally, since every man will frequently find himself coming short of his duty to God and man, and betrayed into sin by the strength of his temptations, his appetites, and passions, in the various occurrences of life, he must repent of his sins, be sincerely sorry for what he has done amiss, humbly ask forgiveness of God, and endeavor to serve and please him in all things for the time to come, and he must exercise a hope or trust in the mercy of God, that upon repentance and new obedience, God will forgive sinners, and take them again into his favor. *Strength and Weakness of Human Reason.*

THE MAN OF HUMILITY

Eudoxus is a gentleman of exalted virtue and unstained reputation; every soul that knows him speaks well of him: he is so much honored, and so well beloved in his nation, that he must flee his country, if he would avoid praises. So sensible is he of the secret pride that has tainted human nature, that he holds himself in perpetual danger, and maintains an everlasting watch. He behaves now with the same modesty as when he was unknown and obscure. He receives the acclamations of the world with such an humble mein, and with such an indifference of spirit, that is truly admirable and divine. It is a lovely pattern, but the imitation is not easy. I took the freedom, one day, to ask him, how he acquired this wondrous humility, or whether he was born with no pride about him? "Ah! no, (said he, with a sacred sigh) I feel the working poison, but I keep my antidote at hand; when my friends tell me of many good qualities and talents, I have learnt from St. Paul to say, *What have I that I have not received?*[1] My own consciousness of many follies and sins constrains me to add, *What have I that I have not misimproved?* And then reason and religion join together to suppress my vanity, and teach me the proper language of a creature and a sinner—*What then have I to glory in?*" *Miscel. Thoughts.*

THE BENEVOLENCE OF THE CREATOR

Upon the whole view of things, I think, from Scripture and reason together, we may justly conclude that where Christ and the gospel are not published, all humble and sincere penitents, asking pardon of God, and hoping in his mercy, (though they know nothing of the particular way or method wherein it is, or has been, or shall

1 1 Corinthians 4:7.

be revealed) shall not fail of pardon and acceptance with God at last, nor miss of some tokens of his favor. This grace has Jesus procured, and God will bestow it. *Strength and Weakness of Human Reason.*

THE GOVERNMENT OF OUR THOUGHTS

There are some thoughts that arise and intrude upon us while we shun them; there are others that fly from us, when we would hold and fix them. If the ideas which you would willingly make the matter of your present meditation are ready to fly from you, you must be obstinate in the pursuit of them by an habit of fixed meditation; you must keep your soul to the work, when it is ready to start aside every moment, unless you will abandon yourself to be a slave to every wild imagination. It is a common, but it is a very unhappy and a shameful thing, that every trifle that comes across the senses or fancy should divert us, that a buzzing fly should tease our spirits, and scatter our best ideas: but we must learn to be deaf to and regardless of other things, besides that which we make the present subject of our meditation; and in order to help a wandering and fickle humor, it is proper to have a book or paper in our hands, which has some proper hints of the subject that we design to pursue. We must be resolute and laborious, and some times conflict with ourselves, if we would be wise and learned.

Yet I would not be too severe in this rule. It must be confessed, there are seasons when the mind, or rather the brain, is over-tired or jaded with study and thinking; or upon some other accounts animal nature may be languid or cloudy, and unfit to assist the spirit in meditation; at such seasons (provided that they return not too often) it is better sometimes to yield to the present indisposition. Then you may think it proper to give yourself up to some hours of leisure and recreation, or *useful* idleness; or if not, then turn your thoughts to some other alluring subject, and pore no longer upon the first, till some brighter or more favorable moments arise. A student shall do more in one hour, when all things concur to invite him to any special study, than in four hours, at a dull and improper season. *Logic.*

OF THE ARRANGEMENT OF OUR IDEAS

As a trader, who never places his goods in his shop or warehouse in a regular order, nor keeps the accounts of his buying and selling, paying and receiving, in a just method, is in the utmost danger of plunging all his affairs into confusion and ruin; so a student who is in search of truth, or an author or teacher who communicates knowledge to others, will very much obstruct his design, and confound his own mind, or the minds of his hearers, unless he range his ideas in just order. If we would therefore become successful learners or teachers, we must not conceive things in a confused heap, but dispose our ideas in some certain method, which may be most easy and useful both for the understanding and memory. *Logic.*

ERRONEOUS JUDGMENT

Where there is wealth, equipage, and splendor, we are ready to call that man happy; but we see not the vexing disquietudes of his soul: and when we spy a person in ragged garments, we form a despicable opinion of him too suddenly; we can hardly think him either happy or wise, our judgment is so biassed by outward and sensible things. It was through the power of this prejudice that the Jews rejected our blessed Saviour; they could not suffer themselves to believe that the man who appeared as the son of a carpenter was also the Son of God. And because St. Paul was of little stature, a mean presence, and his voice contemptible, some of the Corinthians were tempted to doubt whether he was inspired or not. This prejudice is cured by a longer acquaintance with the world, and a just observation that things are sometimes better and sometimes worse than they appear to be. We ought therefore to restrain our excessive forwardness to form our opinion of persons or things before we have opportunity to search into them more perfectly. *Logic.*

There is scarce any thing in the world of nature or art, in the world of morality or religion, that is perfectly uniform. There is a mixture of wisdom and folly, vice and virtue, good and evil, both in men and things. We should remember that some persons have great wit and little judgment; others are judicious but not witty. Some are good humored without compliment; others have all the formality of complaisance, but no good humor. We ought to know that one man may be vicious and learned, while another has virtue without learning; that many a man *thinks* admirably well, who has a poor utterance; while others have a charming manner of speech, but their thoughts are trifling and impertinent. Some are good neighbors, and courteous and charitable towards men, who have no piety towards God; others are truly religious, but of morose natural tempers. Some excellent sayings are found in very silly books, and some silly things appear in books of value. We should neither praise nor dispraise by wholesale, but separate the good from the evil, and judge of them apart: the accuracy of a good judgment consists in making such distinctions. *Logic.*

THE POWER OF ELOQUENCE

When a man of eloquence speaks or writes upon any subject, we are too ready to run into his sentiments, being sweetly and insensibly drawn by the smoothness of his harangue, and the pathetic power of his language. Rhetoric will varnish every error, so that it shall appear in the dress of truth, and put such ornaments upon vice, as to make it look like virtue. It is an art of wondrous and extensive influence; it often conceals, obscures, or overwhelms the truth, and places sometimes a gross falsehood in the most alluring light. The decency of action, the music of the voice, the harmony of the periods, the beauty of the style, and all the engaging airs of the speaker, have often charmed the hearers into error, and persuaded them to approve whatsoever is proposed in so agreeable a manner. A large assembly stands exposed at once to the power of these prejudices, and imbibes them all. So *Cicero* and *Demosthenes* made the Romans and the Athenians believe almost whatsoever they pleased.

The best defense against both these dangers is to learn the skill (as much as possible) of separating our thoughts and ideas from words and phrases, to judge of the things from their own natures, and in their natural or just relation to one another, abstracted from the use of language, and to maintain a steady and obstinate resolution, to hearken to nothing but truth, in whatsoever style or dress it appears. *Logic.*

OBEDIENCE TO THE LAWS

The correction or amendment of the particular offender, is not the only end of punishment, but the vindication of the wisdom and justice of the law-giver and his law, which are like to be insulted, and the laws continually broken afresh, if offenses were always passed by with impunity, and if the criminal were always pardoned upon repentance. It is necessary for a governor sometimes to teach his subjects what an evil thing it is to transgress his law, by the proper punishment of those who offend. The honor and authority of government must be sometimes supported and vindicated by such severities; and though it may please a sovereign sometimes to pardon an offender, out of his great goodness, when he is truly penitent for his crime, yet no degrees of penitence can assure the offender that he shall certainly and entirely be forgiven, or can claim forgiveness at the hands of his sovereign; because repentance makes no recompense at all for the dishonor done to the authority of the law, and of him that made it. His future obedience is all due, if he had never sinned; and therefore it cannot compensate for past neglects and transgressions. *Strength and Weakness of Human Reason.*

SALVATION PROCURED THROUGH THE MEDIATION OF JESUS CHRIST

I am persuaded, that God never did or will forgive the sins of any man upon earth, whether Jew, Heathen, or Christian, nor receive any of our sinful race into his favor, but upon the account of what Jesus Christ his Son, the Mediator, has done and suffered, for the atonement or expiation of sin, and the recovery of man to the favor of God; so that if heathens are saved, I think it is owing to the merit of Christ and his death. *There is salvation in no other, nor is there* <u>*any other name*</u> *whereby men may be saved.*[1] If any of those who

1 Acts 4:12.

never heard of Christ might be saved without the influence of his atonement and mediation, why might not they that have heard of him be saved without it also? Thus there would be no need of him to become a mediator, or to make atonement for the sins of one or the other, and thus Christ would have lived and died to very little purpose. *Strength and Weakness of Human Reason.*

SALVATION TO BE EXTENDED TO THOSE WHO HAVE NOT BELIEVED IN OUR BLESSED SAVIOUR

Though I suppose no man shall be saved but by virtue of the mediation and death of Christ, nor does the gospel permit me to allow salvation to those who wilfully and finally reject it, under clear light and evidence, yet there is good reason to believe, that there have been many sinners actually saved, who never believed in Jesus Christ the Son of Mary, nor ever heard of his name, nor had any notion of his atoning death and sacrifice. Such were some of the early descendants of Noah, who lived long before this name was known in the world, among whom we may reckon Abimelech, king of the Philistines, Melchisedec, king of Salem, Job, in the land of Uz, with his four friends, and many others, who feared God and wrought righteousness: and such were many good men among the Jews, who might be made partakers of the benefits of the death of Christ and his sacrifice, though they had generally no notion of such a sort of Messiah, or Saviour, as was to be made a sacrifice for the sins of men; nor is this at all incredible, since St. Peter himself, who had been a disciple of Christ so long, did not believe this doctrine even a little before his master's death, when he complimented his master concerning his crucifixion, and said, *Be it far from thee, Lord, this shall not be unto thee.*[1]

Nor is it unreasonable to have the same charitable thoughts concerning several other persons of the heathen world, during the continuance of the Jewish church and state, who had either maintained the knowledge of the true God, by tradition from Noah, or

[1] Matthew 16:22.

recovered it by converse with the Jews, and worshipped him as a God of justice and mercy, with fear and hope: such was Cornelius the centurion, and Lydia, and several others, who were called devout persons, and such as feared or worshipped God, in the history of the Acts, chapter 10:7, and 16:14, 17:4, and 10:2. And it is possible, that since the first age of Christianity there may have been some such religious persons, of this same character, who were saved, though they never heard of the doctrine of Jesus Christ; for if they had so much religion as would have saved them before that time, surely they shall never be excluded from salvation for want of hearing of the doctrine of Christ, if they did not lie within the reach of it. *Strength and Weakness of Human Reason.*

BLESSINGS RESULTING FROM PRAYER

There is such a thing as converse with God in prayer, and it is the life and pleasure of a pious soul; without it we are no Christians; and he that practices it most, is the best follower of Christ, for our Lord spent much time in converse with his heavenly Father. This is balm that eases the most raging pains of the mind, when the wounded conscience comes to the mercy-seat, and finds pardon and peace there. This is the cordial that revives and exalts our natures, when the spirit, broken with sorrows, and almost fainting to death, draws near to the almighty Physician, and is healed and refreshed. The mercy-seat in heaven is our surest and sweetest refuge in every hour of distress and darkness upon earth: this is our daily support and relief, while we are passing through a world of temptations and hardships in the way to the promised land. *It is good to draw near to God.*[1] *Sermons, vol.* 1.

LESSON OF HUMILITY

Think what a numberless variety of questions and difficulties there are belonging to that particular science, in which you have made the greatest progress, and how few of them there are in which you have arrived at a final and undoubted certainty, excepting only

1 Psalm 73:28.

those questions in which the pure and simple mathematics, whose theorems are demonstrable, and leave scarce any doubt; and yet even in the pursuit of some few of these mankind have been strangely bewildered.

Spend a few thoughts sometimes on the puzzling inquiries concerning vacuums and atoms, the doctrine of infinites, indivisibles, and incommensurables in geometry, wherein there appear some insolvable difficulties: do this on purpose to give you a more sensible impression of the poverty of your understanding, and the imperfection of your knowledge. This will teach you what a vain thing it is to fancy that you know all things, and will instruct you to think modestly of your present attainments, when every dust of the earth, and every inch of empty space surmounts your understanding, and triumphs over your presumption. *Arithmo* had been bred up to accounts all his life, and thought himself a complete master of numbers. But when he was pushed hard to give the square root of the number 2, he tried at it, and labored long in millesimal fractions, till he confessed there was no end to the inquiry; and yet he learnt so much modesty by this perplexing question, that he was afraid to say, "it was an impossible thing." It is some good degree of improvement when we are afraid to be positive.

Read the accounts of those vast treasures of knowledge which some of the dead have possessed, and some of the living do possess. Read and be astonished at the almost incredible advances which have been made in science. Acquaint yourselves with some persons of great learning, that by converse among them, and comparing yourselves with them, you may acquire a mean opinion of your own attainments, and may thereby be animated with new zeal, to equal them as far as possible, or to exceed: thus let your diligence be quickened by a generous and laudable emulation. *Improvement of the Mind, part* 1.

DOGMATISM CENSURED

Maintain a constant watch at all times against a dogmatical spirit: fix not your assent to any proposition in a firm and unalterable manner, till you have some firm and unalterable ground for it, and till you have arrived at some clear and sure evidence; till you have turned the proposition on all sides, and searched the matter through and through, so that you cannot be mistaken. And even where you think you have full grounds of assurance, be not too early, nor too frequent in expressing this assurance in too peremptory and positive a manner, remembering that human nature is always liable to mistake in this corrupt and feeble state. *Improvement of the Mind, part* 1.

A dogmatical spirit inclines a man to be censorious of his neighbors. Every one of his opinions appears to him written as it were with sunbeams, and he grows angry that his neighbor does not see it in the same light. He is tempted to disdain his correspondents as men of low and dark understandings, because they do not believe what he does. *Improvement of the Mind, part* 1.

MEDITATION

Meditation or study includes all those exercises of the mind whereby we render all the former methods useful for our increase in true knowledge and wisdom. It is by meditation we come to confirm our memory of things that pass through our thoughts in the occurrences of life, in our own experiences, and in the observation we make; it is by meditation that we draw various inferences, and establish in our minds general principles of knowledge; it is by meditation that we compare the various ideas which we derive from our senses, or from the operation of our souls, and join them in propositions. It is by meditation that we fix in our memory whatsoever we learn, and form our own judgment of the truth or falsehood, the strength or weakness of what others speak or write. It is meditation or study that draws out long chains of argument, and searches and finds deep and difficult truths which before lay concealed in darkness. *Improvement of the Mind, part* 1.

OBSERVATION

It is owing to observation that our mind is furnished with the first simple and complex ideas. It is this lays the ground-work and foundation of all knowledge, and makes us capable of using any of the other methods for improving the mind; for if we did not attain a variety of sensible and intellectual ideas, by the sensation of outward objects, by the consciousness of our own appetites and passions, pleasures and pains, and by inward experience of the actings of our own spirits, it would be impossible either for men or books to teach us any thing. It is observation that must give us our first ideas of things, as it includes in it sense and consciousness.

All our knowledge derived from observation, whether it be of single ideas or of propositions, is knowledge gotten at first hand. Hereby we see and know things as they are, or as they appear to us; we take the impressions of them on our minds from the original objects themselves, which give a clearer and stronger conception of things. These ideas are more lively, and the propositions (at least in many cases) are much more evident; whereas what knowledge we derive from lectures, reading, and conversation, is but the copy of other men's ideas; that is, the picture of a picture; and it is one remove further from the original.

Another advantage of observation is, that we may gain knowledge all the day long, and every moment of our lives; and every moment of our existence we may be adding something to our intellectual treasures thereby, except only while we are asleep; and even then the remembrance of our dreamings will teach us some truths, and lay a foundation for a better acquaintance with human nature, both in the powers and in the frailties of it. *Improvement of the Mind, part* 1.

ADVANTAGES OF READING

By reading we acquaint ourselves, in a very extensive manner, with the affairs, actions, and thoughts of the living and the dead, in the most remote nations, and in the most distant ages; and that with as much ease as though they lived in our own age and nation. By reading of books we may learn something from all parts of mankind; whereas by observation we learn all from ourselves, and only what comes within our own direct cognizance: by conversation we can only enjoy the assistance of a very few persons, *viz.* those who are near us, and live at the same time that we do; that is, our neighbors and contemporaries. But our knowledge is still much more narrowed than if we confine ourselves merely to our own solitary reasonings, without much observation or reading; for then all our improvement must arise only from our own inward powers and meditations. *Improvement of the Mind, part* 1.

READING AND CONVERSATION CONTRASTED

By reading we learn not only the actions and the sentiments of distant nations and ages, but we transfer to ourselves the knowledge and improvements of the most learned men, and the wisest and the best of mankind, when or wheresoever they lived: for though many books have been written by weak and injudicious persons, yet the most of those books which have obtained great reputation in the world, are the products of great and wise men in their several ages and nations; whereas we can obtain the conversation and instruction of those only who are within the reach of our dwelling, or our acquaintance, whether they are wise or unwise; and sometimes that narrow sphere scarce affords any person of great eminence in wisdom or learning, unless our instructor happen to have this character. And as for our own studies and meditations, even when we arrive at some good degrees of learning, our advantage for further improvement in knowledge by them is still far more contracted than what we may derive from reading.

When we read good authors, we learn the best, the most labored, and most refined sentiments even of those wise and learned men; for they have studied hard, and committed to writing their maturest thoughts, and the result of their long study and experience; whereas by conversation, and in some lectures, we obtain many times only the present thoughts of our tutors or friends, which (though they may be bright and useful) yet, at first, perhaps, may be sudden and indigested, and are mere hints, which have risen to no maturity.

It is another advantage of reading, that we may review what we have read; we may consult the page again and again, and meditate on it, at successive seasons, in our serenest and retired hours, having the book always at hand; but what we obtain by conversation, and in lectures, is oftentimes lost again as soon as the company breaks up, or at least when the day vanishes, unless we happen to have the talent of a good memory, or quickly retire and mark down what *remarkables* we have found in those discourses. And for the same reason, and for want of retiring and writing, many a learned man has lost several useful meditations of his own, and could never recall them again. *Improvement of the Mind, part* 1.

VERBAL INSTRUCTION

There is something more sprightly, more delightful and entertaining in the living discourse of a wise, a learned, and well qualified teacher, than there is in the silent and sedentary practice of reading. The very turn of voice, the good pronunciation, and the polite and alluring manner which some teachers have attained, will engage the attention, keep the soul fixed, and convey and insinuate into the mind the ideas of things in a more lively and forcible way, than the mere reading of books in the silence and retirement of the closet. *Improvement of the Mind, part* 1.

CONVERSATION

When we converse familiarly with a learned friend, we have his own help at hand to explain to us every word and sentiment that seems obscure in his discourse, and to inform us of his whole meaning, so that we are in much less danger of mistaking his sense; whereas in books, whatsoever is really obscure, may also abide always obscure without remedy, since the author is not at hand, that we may inquire his sense.

If we mistake the meaning of our friend in conversation, we are quickly set right again; but in reading we many times go on in the same mistake, and are not capable of recovering ourselves from it.

Thence it comes to pass that we have so many contests in all ages about the meaning of ancient authors, and especially sacred writers. Happy should we be, could we but converse with Moses, Isaiah and St. Paul, and consult the prophets and apostles, when we meet with a difficult text! But that glorious conversation is reserved for the ages of future blessedness. *Improvement of the Mind, part* 1.

Conversation calls out into light what has been lodged in all the recesses and secret chambers of the soul. By occasional hints and incidents it brings old useful notions into remembrance; it unfolds and displays the hidden treasures of knowledge with which reading, observation and study had before furnished the mind. By mutual discourse, the soul is awakened and allured to bring forth its hoards of knowledge, and it learns how to render them most useful to mankind. A man of vast reading without conversation, is like a miser who lives only to himself.

In free and friendly conversation our intellectual powers are more animated, and our spirits act with a superior vigor in the quest and pursuit of unknown truths. There is a sharpness and sagacity of thought that attends conversation beyond what we find while we are shut up reading and musing in our retirements. Our souls may be serene in solitude, but not sparkling, though perhaps we are employed in reading the works of the brightest writers. Often has it happened in free discourse, that new thoughts are strangely struck out and the seeds of truth sparkle and blaze through the company, which in calm and silent reading would never have been excited. By conversation you will both give and receive this benefit; as flints, when put into motion, and striking against each other, produce a living fire on both sides, which would never have risen from the same hard materials in a state of rest.

In generous conversation among ingenious and learned men, we have a great advantage of proposing our own opinions, and of bringing our own sentiments to the test, and learning in a more compendious way what the world will judge of them, how mankind will receive them, what objections may be raised against them, what defects there are in our scheme, and how to correct our own mistakes; which advantages are not so easy obtained by our own private meditations: for the pleasure we take in our own notions, and the passion of self-love, as well as the narrowness of our own views, tempts us to pass too favorable an opinion of our own schemes; whereas the variety of genius in our several associates, will give happy notices how our opinion will stand in the view of mankind.

It is also another considerable advantage of conversation, that it furnishes the student with the knowledge of men and the affairs of life, as reading furnishes him with book-learning. A man who dwells all his days among books, may have amassed together a vast heap of notions, but he may be a mere scholar, which is a contemptible sort of character in the world. A hermit who has been shut up in his cell in a college, has contracted a sort of mold and rust upon his soul, and all his airs of behavior have a certain awkwardness in them: but these awkward airs are worn off by degrees in company: the rust and the mold are filed and brushed off by polite conversation. The scholar now becomes a citizen or a gentleman, a neighbor and a friend; he learns how to dress his sentiments in the fairest colors, as well as to set them in the fairest light. Thus he brings out his notions with honor, he makes some use of them in the world, and improves the theory by practice. *Improvement of the Mind, part 1.*

HATRED REPROVED, AND LOVE OF OUR FELLOW CREATURES RECOMMENDED

Consider whether the persons you hate are good or not. If they are good and pious, your hatred has a double guilt in it, since you are bound to love them both as men and Christians. Will you hate those whom God loves? Will you hate those who have the image of Christ, and in whom the Spirit of God inhabits? If they have any blamable qualities in them, let your charity cover those faults and follies: let your thoughts rather dwell upon their virtues, and their sacred relation to God. This will have a happy influence to turn your hatred into love. Think of them as members of Christ, and you cannot hate them if you are of that blessed body.

If they are persons who neglect religion, and have not the fear of God, yet they may have some good qualities in them, some moral or social virtues, or some natural excellencies which may merit your esteem, and invite your love: at least these agreeable qualities may diminish your aversion, and abate your hatred. I confess it is the nature of malice and envy, to overlook all that is good and amiable in a person, and to remark only what is evil and hateful: but this is not the spirit and temper of a Christian, nor of Jesus Christ our master. There was a young man who loved his riches so well, that he refused to become a disciple; yet our blessed Lord saw some good qualities in him; *he looked upon him, and loved him.*[1]

But if the persons whom you hate have nothing good in them that you can find, then they ought to be pitied rather than to be hated; they are not worthy of your envy, nor do they need the punishment of your malice in this world, who expose themselves to the wrath and vengeance of God in the world to come.

Will you say, they are so impious before God, and so injurious to man, that they deserve to be hated? But consider, if you were but punished in respect as you deserve, both for your offenses against God and man, what would become of you? Pity them, therefore, as you hope for pity. Imitate the goodness of *your heavenly Father, who makes his sun to shine, and his rain to fall on the just and on the unjust.*[2] This is the rule of Christ. *Doctrine of the Passions.*

FEAR

Fear is a powerful and useful passion, to guard us from mischief and misery, to hasten our avoidance of every danger, to drive us to our refuge, and to restrain us from every thing which has a tendency to bring the evil or mischief upon us.

The anger of God is the most proper object of our fear, as we are sinful creatures; nor can sinners fear the anger of God too much,

---

1 Mark 10:21.
2 Matthew 5:45.

until they have complied with the appointed methods of his grace. There is also a reverence and holy fear due to the majesty of God, even when we have obtained the most solid hopes of his mercy: we must always fear to sin against God, and keep up a holy jealousy of all temptations to sin. All this is called religious fear. *Doctrine of the Passions.*

UNREASONABLE FEAR

But the fear which I speak of in this place is an unjust and unreasonable fear of any creature whatsoever, or of any occurrences in life: it is a timorous spirit, which subjects the whole nature to the power and tyranny of the passion of fear beyond all reasonable grounds; as for instance, a fear of being alone, or in the dark; a perpetual fear of evil accidents by fire or water or wicked men; a disquieting fear of ghosts and apparitions; of little inconsiderable animals, such as spiders, frogs, or worms; unreasonable and anxious fears of the loss of estate or friends; fear of poverty or calamity of any kind, whereby we are too often restrained from our present duty, and our lives are made very uncomfortable. All manner of fear becomes irregular when it rises to an excessive degree, and is superior to the danger. *Doctrine of the Passions.*

AGAINST HASTY DETERMINATION

A hasty determination of some universal principles without a due survey of all the particular cases which may be included in them, is the way to lay a trap for our own understandings in the pursuit of any subject, and we shall often be taken captives into mistake and falsehood. *Improvement of the Mind, part* 1.

PROFITABLE METHOD OF READING
RECOMMENDED

Books of importance of any kind, and especially complete treatises on any subject, should be first read in a more general and cursory manner, to learn a little what the treatise promises, and what you may expect from the writer's manner and skill. And for this end I would advise always that the preface be read, and a survey taken of the table of contents, if there be one, before this first survey of the book. By this means you will not only be better fitted to give the book the first reading, but you will be much assisted in your second perusal of it, which should be done with greater attention and deliberation, and you will learn with more ease and readiness what the author pretends to teach. In your reading, *mark* what is new or unknown to you before, and review those chapters, pages, or paragraphs. Unless a reader has an uncommon and most retentive memory, I may venture to affirm, that there is scarce any book or chapter worth reading once, that is not worthy a second perusal. At least take a careful review of all the lines or paragraphs which you *marked*, and make a recollection of the sections which you thought truly valuable.

There is another reason also why I would choose to take a superficial and cursory survey of a book before I sit down to read it, and dwell upon it with studious attention; and that is, that there may be several difficulties in it which we cannot easily understand and conquer at the first reading, for want of a fuller comprehension of the author's whole scheme. And therefore in such treatises we should not stay till we master *every* difficulty at the first perusal; for, perhaps, many of these would appear to be solved when we have proceeded farther in the book, or would vanish of themselves upon a second reading.

What we cannot reach and penetrate at first, may be noted down as a matter of after consideration and inquiry, if the pages that follow do not happen to strike a complete light upon these that went before. *Improvement of the Mind, part* 1.

BENEFIT OF CONVERSING WITH MEN OF VARIOUS COUNTRIES, AND OF DIFFERENT PARTIES OPINIONS, AND PRACTICES

Confine not yourself always to one sort of company, or to persons of the same party or opinion, either in matters of learning, religion, or the civil life; lest if you should happen to be nursed up or educated in early mistake, you should be confirmed and established in the same mistake, by conversing only with persons of the same sentiments. A free and general conversation with men of very various countries, and of different parties, opinions, and practices, (so far as may be done safely) is of excellent use to undeceive us in many wrong judgments which we may have framed, and to lead us into juster thoughts. It is said, when the king of Siam, near China, first conversed with some European merchants, who sought the favor of trading on his coast, he inquired of them some of the common appearances of summer and winter in their country; and when they told him of water growing so hard in their rivers, that men and horses, and laden carriages passed over it, and that rain sometimes fell down as white and light as feathers, and sometimes almost as hard as stones, he could not believe a syllable they said, for ice, snow, and hail, were names and things utterly unknown to him, and to his subjects in that hot climate; he therefore renounced all traffic with such shameful liars, and would not suffer them to trade with his people. See here the natural effects of gross ignorance.

Conversation with foreigners, on various occasions, has a happy influence to enlarge our minds, and to set them free from many errors and gross prejudices we are ready to imbibe concerning them. *Improvement of the Mind, part* 1.

TO RENDER CONVERSATION INSTRUCTIVE

To make conversation more valuable and useful, whether it be in a designed or accidental visit, among persons of the same or different sexes, after the necessary salutations are finished, and the stream of common talk begins to hesitate, or runs flat and low, let some one person take a book which may be agreeable to the whole company, and by common consent let him read in it ten lines, or a paragraph or two, or a few pages, till some word or sentence gives occasion for any of the company to offer a thought or two relating to that subject: interruption of the reader should be no blame, for conversation is the business; whether it be to confirm what the author says or to improve it, to enlarge upon it or to correct it, to object against it or to ask any question that is akin to it; and let every one that please add their opinion, and promote the conversation. When the discourse sinks again, or diverts to trifles, let him that reads pursue the page, and read on further paragraphs or pages, till some occasion is given by a word or a sentence for a new discourse to be started, and that with the utmost ease and freedom. Such a method as this would prevent the hours of a visit from running all to waste; and by this means even among scholars, they will seldom find occasion for that too just and bitter reflection, "I have lost my time in the company of the learned."

By such practice as this is, young ladies may very honorably and agreeably improve their hours, while one applies herself to reading, the others employ their attention, even among the various artifices of the needle; but let all of them make their occasional remarks or inquiries. This will guard a good deal of that precious time from modish trifling impertinence or scandal, which might otherwise afford matter for painful repentance.

Observe this rule in general: whensoever it lies in your power to lead the conversation, let it be directed to some profitable point of knowledge or practice, so far as may be done with decency; and let not the discourse and the hours be suffered to run loose without aim or design: and when a subject is started, pass not hastily to another, before you have brought the present theme of discourse to some tolerable issue, or a joint consent to drop it. *Improvement of the Mind, part* 1.

EXHORTATION AGAINST EXCESSIVE SORROW

Let not your thoughts dwell continually upon your distresses and afflictions. Suffer not the chambers of your soul to be ever hung round with dark and dismal ideas; chew not always the wormwood and the gall; but remember the many temporal mercies you enjoy, and the rich treasures of grace in the gospel. Survey the immortal blessings of pardon of sin, and eternal life; the love of God, and the hope of heaven. Look sometimes on those brighter scenes; suffer not your sorrow to bury all your past and present comforts in darkness and oblivion. Thankfulness is one way to joy.

Remember, if you are a Christian indeed, the springs of your grief cannot flow long; the hour of death will dry them all up. The last moment of this mortal life is a certain and final period to sorrow. Converse much among the mansions and joys of the invisible world, and your hope which is laid up there: the very gleamings of that glory will brighten the darkest providences, and relieve the soul under its sharpest pains.

Compare your miseries with your sins, and then you will think them lighter. You will learn then to bear your burdens with a more serene and peaceful mind, and turn your sorrows into repentance for sin. But, alas! we aggravate our sufferings, and extenuate and excuse our sins: whereas sufferings would appear lighter, if we did but consider how much heavier evils we have deserved from the hands of a holy and offended God. *Doctrine of the Passions.*

DISPUTATION

Great care must be taken, lest your debates break in upon your passions, and awaken them to take part in the controversy. When the opponent pushes hard and gives just and mortal wounds to our own opinion, our passions are very apt to feel the strokes, and to rise in resentment and defense. *Self* is so mingled with the sentiments which we have chosen, and has such a tender feeling of all the opposition which is made to them, that personal brawls are very ready to come in as seconds to succeed and finish the dispute of opinions. Then noise, and clamor, and folly, appear in all their shapes, and chase reason and truth out of sight. *Improvement of the Mind.*

ACADEMICAL DISPUTATIONS

It must be confessed there are some advantages to be attained by academical disputation. It gives vigor and briskness to the mind thus exercised, and relieves the languor of private study and meditation. It sharpens the wit and all the inventive powers. It makes the thoughts active, and sends them on all sides to find arguments and answers both for opposition and defense. It gives opportunity of viewing the subject of discourse on all sides, and of learning what inconveniences, difficulties and objections attend particular opinions. It furnishes the soul with various occasions of starting such thoughts as otherwise would never have come into the mind. It makes a student more expert in attacking and refuting an error, as well as in vindicating a truth. It instructs a scholar in the various methods of warding off the force of objections, and of discovering and repelling the subtle tricks of sophisters. It procures also a freedom and readiness of speech, and raises the modest and diffident genius to a due degree of courage.

But there are some very grievous inconveniences that may sometimes overbalance all these advantages. For many young students, by a constant habit of disputing, grow impudent and audacious, proud and disdainful, talkative and impertinent, and render themselves intolerable by an obstinate humor of maintaining whatsoever they have asserted, as well as by a spirit of contradiction, opposing almost every thing they hear. The disputation itself often awakens the passions of ambition, emulation, and anger: it carries away the mind from that calm and sedate temper which is so necessary to contemplate truth. *Improvement of the Mind, part* 1.

OF FIXING THE ATTENTION

A student should labor by all proper methods to acquire a steady fixation of thought. Attention is a very necessary thing in order to improve our minds. The evidence of truth does not always appear immediately, nor strike the soul at first sight. It is by long attention and inspection that we arrive at evidence, and it is for want of it that we judge falsely of many things. We make haste to judge and determine upon a slight and sudden view; we confirm our guesses which arise from a glance; we pass a judgment while we have but a confused or obscure perception, and thus plunge ourselves into mistakes. This is like a man, who, walking in a mist, or being at a great distance from any visible object, (suppose a tree, a man, a horse, or a church) judges much amiss of the figure, and situation, and colors of it, and sometimes takes one for the other; whereas if he would but withhold his judgment till he comes nearer to it, or stay till clearer light comes, and then would fix his eyes longer upon it, he would secure himself from those mistakes. *Improvement of the Mind, part* 1.

Mathematical studies have a strange influence towards fixing the attention of the mind, and giving a steadiness to a wandering disposition, because they deal much in lines, figures, and numbers, which affect and please the sense and imagination. Histories have a strong tendency the same way; for they engage the soul by a variety of sensible occurrences; when it has begun, it knows not how to leave off; it longs to know the final event through a natural curiosity that belongs to mankind. Voyages and travels and accounts of strange countries and strange appearances, will assist in this work. This sort of study detains the mind by the perpetual occurrence and expectation of something new, and that which may gratefully strike the imagination. *Improvement of the Mind, part* 1.

OF SCIENCE

The best way to learn any science is to begin with a regular system, or a short and plain scheme of that science, well drawn up into a narrow compass, omitting the deep or more abstruse parts of it, and that also under the conduct and instruction of some skillful teacher. Systems are necessary to give an entire and comprehensive view of the several parts of any science, which may have a mutual influence towards the application or proof of each other: whereas if a man deals always and only in essays, and discourses on particular parts of a science, he will never obtain a distinct and just idea of the whole, and may perhaps omit some important part of it, after seven years reading of such occasional discourses. For this reason, young students should apply themselves to their systems much more than pamphlets. That man is never fit to judge of particular subjects relating to any science, who has never taken a survey of the whole.

It is the remark of an ingenious writer, should a barbarous Indian, who had never seen a palace or a ship, view their separate and disjointed parts, and observe the pillars, doors, windows, cornices, and turrets of the one, or the prow and stern, the ribs and masts, the rope and shrouds, the sails and tackle of the other, he would be able to form but a very lame and dark idea of either of those excellent and useful inventions. In like manner, those who contemplate only the fragments or pieces broken off from any science, dispersed in short unconnected discourses, and do not discern their relation to each other, and how they may be adapted, and by their union procure the delightful symmetry of a regular scheme, can never survey an entire body of truth, but must always view it as deformed and distempered; while their ideas, which must be ever indistinct and often repugnant, will lie in the brain unsorted, and thrown together without order or coherence: such is the knowledge of those men who live upon the scraps of science. *Improvement of the Mind, part* 1.

REASON, A PRINCIPAL SOURCE OF RELIGION

Human reason is the first ground and spring of all human religion. Man is obliged to religion because he is a reasonable creature. Reason directs and obliges us not only to search out and practice the will of God, as far as natural conscience will lead us, but also to examine, receive, and obey, all the revelations which come from God, where we are placed within the reach of their proper evidences. Whereinsoever revelation gives us plain and certain rules for our conduct, reason itself obliges us to submit and follow them. Where the rules of duty are more obscure, we are to use our reason to find them out, as far as we can, by comparing one part of revelation with another, and making just and reasonable inferences from the various circumstances and connections of things. In those parts or circumstances of religion where revelation is silent, there we are called to betake ourselves to reason again as our best guide and conductor. *Rational Found of a Christian Church.*

PUBLIC ADORATION OF THE ALMIGHTY

The several acts of worship which the light of nature directs us to pay to the great God, are such as these: To adore him with all humility, on the account of his glorious perfections, and his wonderful works of power and wisdom; to join together in prayer to God for such blessings as we stand in need of; to confess our sins, and ask the forgiveness of them; to acknowledge his mercies, and give thanks to his goodness; and to sing with the voice to his honor and praise.

The light of nature directs us also to seek continually a further acquaintance with the nature and will of that God whom we worship, in order to practice our duty the better, and please our Creator, and to provide some way for the further instruction of those who are ignorant of that religion, and to come into their assemblies to be instructed; and for the exhortation of the people to fulfill their duty to God and their neighbors. And if there are any special rights or ceremonies, such as belong to social worship, the light of nature tells us, that here they ought to be performed.

And does not the New Testament set all these matters before us so plainly and frequently, with regard to Christianity, that I need not stand to cite chapter and verse, where these things are practiced by the apostles and the primitive Christians, in their assemblies? Here adoration, prayer, and thanksgivings, are offered up to God, but in the name of Jesus, as their only mediator: here their addresses are made to God, with one mind, and with one mouth, to the glory of God, who is the God and Father of our Lord Jesus Christ: here psalms, and hymns, and spiritual songs, are sung to the honor of the Creator and Redeemer: here the Word of God is preached for the instruction of the ignorant or unbelievers, who come into the Christian assemblies, that sinners or infidels may be converted, and Christians edified and exhorted to persist in the faith and improve in holiness.[1] Here the great ordinance of Christian Communion, the Lord's Supper, is celebrated, by distributing and receiving bread

1 1 Corinthians 14:23.

and wine, and eating and drinking in remembrance of their common Saviour, and his death.[1] As for the other ordinance, *viz.* baptism, it being not so properly an act of public or social religion, I do not find it is any where required to be done in public; and though it might be rendered more extensively useful by that means for some purposes, yet it may be performed in private houses, or in retired places, as it was in the primitive ages. *Rational Found of a Christian Church.*

THAT PROVISION SHOULD BE MADE FOR THE SUPPORT OF THE MINISTERS OF THE GOSPEL

Though Christian ministers should be supported in temporal things, that they may not labor under perpetual cares, and daily anxieties, how to get bread and raiment for themselves and their families, and that they may maintain their proper authority in preaching, reproving, and exhorting, and live above the fear or shame that may arise from poverty and dishonorable dependences, yet there is no rule nor example in Scripture that should raise them so far above the people in riches or grandeur, as to become the lords of God's heritage, or tempt them to assume sovereign dominion over the conscience, faith, or practice. *Rational Found of a Christian Church.*

THE DUTY OF CHRISTIAN MINISTERS

The rule and government which is committed to ordinary ministers in the church, so far as I can understand it, seems to consist in these things following, *viz.* In going before the people, and leading the several parts of their worship, and becoming their example in every duty; in teaching them the principles and rules of their religion; the knowledge, profession and practice of those doctrines and duties, that worship and order, which reason and natural religion dictate, and that which Christ himself has revealed, superadded, and established in his word: it consists in exhorting, persuading, and charging the hearers with solemnity, in the name and

1 1 Corinthians 11:20, etc.

authority of Christ, to comply therewith; in instructing the people
how to apply these general principles and rules to particular cases
and occurrences, and giving them their best advice; in presiding
in their assemblies; and particularly as to the admission and exclu-
sion of members: it consists in watching over the flock; in guard-
ing them against errors and dangers; in admonishing, and warning,
and reproving, with all gravity and authority, those who neglect
or oppose the rules of Christ. But I cannot find where our blessed
Lord has given them any power, or pretence of power, to impose on
conscience any such advices of their own, which neither reason nor
revelation impose; much less to impose any of their own inventions
of new doctrine, or duties; or so much as their own peculiar explications of the words of Christ, by their own authority. When our
Saviour gave commission to his disciples, or his apostles, to *"preach
the gospel to all nations,"* it was in this manner; *"Go teach them to
observe"* (not whatsoever you shall command, but) *"whatsoever I
have commanded you."*[1] *Rational Found of a Christian Church.*

RELIGIOUS LIBERTY

A Christian church allows all its members the most perfect liberty of men and Christians. It is inconsistent with persecution for
conscience sake; for it leaves all civil rewards and punishments to
kingdoms, and states, and the governors of this world. It pretends to
no power over conscience, to compel men to obedience; no prisons,
no axes, fire nor sword. It gives its ministers power and authority to
command nothing but what is found in the Bible. *Rational Found
of a Christian Church.*

If any person sins so grossly against the plain rules of the gospel, or the laws of God and Christ, as to appear to renounce the
characters of a Christian, the church has power only to renounce
such a person, and disclaim all Christian fellowship with him, and
to turn him into the world, which is the kingdom of Satan, till he
repent: but they have no authority to hurt his life or limbs; to touch

---

1 Matthew 28:19, 20.

a hair of his head, nor a penny of his money, by way of punishment. *Rational Found of a Christian Church.*

A professor of every religion has a right to be protected by the government, as long as he maintains his allegiance to the governors, and does no injury to the state. But if governors will not protect him, but will give him up to the fury of persecutors, he has certainly a civil right to defend himself and his friends against all assaults and injuries. *Rational Found of a Christian Church.*

THE PREJUDICE OF CREDULITY, AND A SPIRIT OF CONTRADICTION CONTRASTED

The credulous man is ready to receive every thing for truth, that has but the shadow of evidence; every new book that he reads, and every ingenious man with whom he converses, has power enough to draw him into the sentiments of the speaker or writer. He has so much complaisance in him, or weakness of soul, that he is ready to resign his own opinion to the first objection which he hears, and to receive any sentiments of another that are asserted with a positive air and much assurance. Thus he is under a kind of necessity, through the indulgence of this credulous humor, either to be often changing his opinions, or to believe inconsistencies.

The man of contradiction is of a very contrary humor; for he stands ready to oppose everything that is said: he gives but a slight attention to the reasons of other men, from an inward scornful presumption that they have no strength in them. When he reads or hears a discourse different from his own sentiments, he does not give himself leave to consider, whether that discourse may be true; but employs all his powers immediately to confute it. Your great disputers, and your men of controversy, are in continual danger of this sort of prejudice: they contend often for victory, and will maintain whatsoever they have asserted, while truth is lost in the noise and tumult of reciprocal contradictions; and it frequently happens, that a debate about opinions is turned into a mutual reproach of persons. *Logic.*

RULES FOR CORRECTING CREDULOUS AND CONTRADICTORY DISPOSITIONS

The prejudice of credulity may in some measure be cured, by learning to set a high value upon truth, and by taking more pains to attain it; remembering that truth often lies dark and deep, and requires us to dig for it as hid treasure; and that falsehood often puts on a fair disguise, and therefore we should not yield up our judgment to every plausible appearance. It is no part of civility or good breeding to part with truth, but to maintain it with decency and candor.

A spirit of contradiction is so pedantic and hateful, that a man should take much pains with himself to watch against every instance of it; he should learn so much good humor, at least, as never to oppose any thing without just and solid reason for it: he should abate some degrees of pride and moroseness, which are never-failing ingredients in this sort of temper, and should seek after so much honesty and conscience, as never to contend for conquest or triumph; but to review his own reasons, and to read the arguments of his opponents, if possible, with an equal indifference, be glad to spy a truth, and to submit to it, though it appear on the opposite side. *Logic.*

THE INFLUENCE OF CUSTOM

Suppose we have freed ourselves from the younger prejudices of our education, yet we are in danger of having our mind turned aside from truth by the influence of general custom. Our opinion of meats and drinks, of garments and forms of salutation, are influenced more by custom, than by the eye, the ear, or the taste. Custom prevails even over sense itself, and therefore no wonder if it prevail over reason too. What is it but custom that renders many of the mixtures of food and sauces elegant in Britain, which would be awkward and nauseous to the inhabitants of China, and indeed were nauseous to us when we first tasted them? What but custom could make those salutations polite in Muscovy, which are ridiculous in

France and England? We call ourselves indeed the politer nations, but it is *we* who judge thus of ourselves; and that fancied politeness is oftentimes more owing to custom than reason. Why are the forms of our present garments counted beautiful, and those fashions of our ancestors the matter of scoff and contempt, which in their days were all decent and genteel? It is custom that forms our opinion of dress, and reconciles us by degrees to those habits which at first seemed very odd and monstrous. It must be granted, there are some garments and habits which have a natural congruity or incongruity, modesty or immodesty, gaudery or gravity; though for the most part there is but little reason in these affairs; but what little there is of reason or natural decency, custom triumphs over it all. It is almost impossible to persuade a young lady that any thing can be decent which is out of fashion.

The methods of our education are governed by custom. It is custom, and not reason, that sends every boy to learn the Roman poets, and begin a little acquaintance with Greek, before he is bound apprentice to a soap-boiler or a leather-seller. It is custom alone that teaches us Latin by the rules of a Latin grammar; a tedious and absurd method! And what is it but custom that has for past centuries confined the brightest geniuses, even of the highest rank in the female world, to the business of the needle only, and secluded them most unmercifully from the pleasures of knowledge, and the divine improvements of reason. But we begin to break all these chains, and reason begins to dictate the education of youth. *Logic.*

ABSURDITY OF HEREDITARY PREJUDICES EXPOSED

Some persons believe every thing that their kindred, their parents, and their tutors believe. The veneration and the love which they have for their ancestors, incline them to swallow down all their opinions at once, without examining what truth or falsehood there is in them. Men take their principles by inheritance, and defend them as they would their estates, because they are born heirs to them. I freely grant, that parents are appointed by God and nature to teach us all the sentiments and practices of our younger years; and happy are those whose parents lead them into the paths of wisdom and truth. I grant further, that when persons come to years of discretion, and judge for themselves, they ought to examine the opinions of their parents, with the greatest modesty, and with an humble deference to their superior character; they ought, in matters perfectly dubious, to give the preference to their parents' advice, and always to pay them the first respect, nor ever depart from their opinions and practices, till reason and conscience make it necessary. But after all, it is possible that parents may be mistaken, and therefore reason and Scripture ought to be our final rules of determination in matters that relate to this world, and that which is to come. *Logic.*

OPPOSITE DUTIES

Where two duties seem to stand in opposition to each other, and we cannot practice both, the less must give way to the greater, and the omission of the less is not sinful. So ceremonial laws give way to moral. *God will have mercy and not sacrifice. Logic.*

ABSENCE FROM GOD WHO IS OUR ALL

My God, my Maker, I have called thee my all-satisfying portion, and my eternal good. When I contemplate thee, I stand amazed at thy grandeur; thy wisdom, thy power, thy fullness of blessing, wrap my soul up in astonishment and devout silence. In that happy moment my soul cries out, what are creatures when compared with thee, but mere shadows of being and faint reflections of thy light and beauty! And yet, stupid as I am, I soon lose my sight of God, and stand gazing upon thy creatures all the day, as if beauty and light were theirs in the original.

What are they all, O my God, but empty cisterns that can give no relief to a thirsty soul, unless thou supply them with rivulets from on high? And yet we crowd about these cisterns, and are attached to them, as though they were the unfailing springs and fountains of our blessedness. Every breath we draw is a new and unmerited gift from heaven; God is *our life and the length of our days;* and yet we are contented to spend that life far from heaven and from God, and to dwell afar off from him, amidst the regions of mortality and death: we are ever grovelling in this land of graves, as though immortal blessings were to be drawn from the clods of it.

Our real and eternal interest depends more on thy single favor, than on the united friendship of the whole creation; and yet, foolish wanderers that we are! We absent ourselves from our God, and rove far and wide to seek interests and friendships among creatures whose character is weakness, vanity, and disappointing vexation. How fond are we of a word or a look from a worm in a high station? How do we caress them and court their love, at the expense of virtue and truth, and the favor of God our Maker? And yet they are nothing without God; but he is our all without their leave.

Should my father, and my mother, and every mortal friend forsake me, and every good angel take his flight; should these heavens and this earth, with all their innumerable inhabitants, disappear at once, and vanish into their first nothing; thy presence with me is all-sufficient, thy hand would support my being, and thy love would furnish out an eternity of life and coeval happiness. Why then do I tie myself so fast to my mortal friends, as though my separation from them were certain misery? Why do I lean upon creatures with my whole weight, as though nothing else could support me?

Oh my God! I am convinced that I have more affairs, and of far higher importance to transact with thee, than with all thy creatures, and yet I am ever chattering with thy creatures, and say little to my God; or at best give him a morning or an evening salutation, and perhaps too with indolence and formality. *Whom have I in heaven or on earth but thee,*[1] that can supply all my wants, and fill up all the vacancies of my heart? And yet how are my thoughts and hours busily employed in quest of satisfaction among the shining snares, or at best among the flattering impertinences of the world; though every new experiment shows me they are all unsatisfying?

1 Psalm 73:25.

If I happen to find anything here below made a channel to convey some blessing to me from thy hand, how prone am I to make an idol of it, and place it in the room of my God?

How much, alas! do I trust to my food to nourish, and physic to heal me! but it is thou alone canst bless me with ease, nourishment, and health, while I dwell in this cottage of flesh and blood. Let medicines and physicians pronounce despair and death upon me, a word of thine can shut the mouth of the grave, can renew the vigor and bloom of youth, and repair the decays of nature. If thou withhold thy vital influence, my flesh languishes and expires even among the luxurious provisions of the table, and the recipes of the learned; and it is thou only canst provide me a blissful habitation when this cottage is fallen to the ground. *Father, into thy hand I commend my spirit,* when it is dislodged from this mortal tabernacle; and why should I not keep my spirit ever near thee, since every moment I am liable to be turned out of this dwelling, and sent a naked stranger into the unknown world of spirits?

It is but a few days and nights more that I can have to do with sun, moon, and stars; a little time will finish all my commerce with this visible world; but I have affairs of infinite and everlasting moment to transact with the great God. It is before thy tribunal I must stand, as the final judge of all my conduct, from whose decisive sentence there is no appeal; and yet how fond am I, and wretchedly solicitous, to approve myself rather to creatures whose opinion and sentence is but empty air. It is by thy judgment that I must stand or fall forever; the words of thy lips, will be my eternal bliss, or my everlasting woe; why then should I, a little insect, or atom of being, be concerned about the smiles or frowns of my fellow insects, my equal atoms? Can all their applauses, or their reproaches, weigh a grain in the divine balance, that sacred and tremendous balance of divine justice, in which all my actions and my soul itself must be weighed? Let all the creatures above and below frown and scowl upon me; if my Creator smile, I am happy; nor can all their frownings diminish my complete joy.

Forgive, gracious God, forgive the past follies and wanderings of a sinful worm, from thee the highest and best of beings. I am even amazed at my own stupidity, that I could live so much absent from thee, when my eternal all depends upon thee.

And how much more inexcusable is my forgetfulness of my God, since he has sent his own Son, his fairest image, into flesh and blood, to put me in mind of my maker, and to teach me what my God is? *He that has seen me,* says he, *has seen the Father,*[1] *I and the Father are one.* We happen to be born indeed too late for the sight of his face, but we have the transcript of his heart, the true copy of his life, and the very features of his soul, conveyed down to us in his ever-living gospels. There we may read *Jesus,* there we may learn the *Father.* O may the little remnant of my days be spent in the presence of my God; and when I am constrained to converse with creatures, let me ever remember that I have infinitely more to do with my Creator, and thus shorten my talk and traffic with them, that I may have leisure to converse the longer with thee. Let me see thee in every thing; let me read thy name every where; sounds, shapes, colors, motions, and all visible things, let them all teach me an invisible God. Let creatures be nothing to me, but as the books which thou has lent me to instruct me in the lessons of thy power, wisdom, and love; above all let me derive this science by converse with the blessed *Jesus,* and may I be so wise a proficient in this divine school, as to learn some new lesson daily. Train me up among thy visible works and thy Word, O my heavenly Father, by the condescending methods of thy grace and providence, until I am loosened and weaned from all things below God; and then give me a glorious dismission into that intellectual and blissful world where, in a more immediate manner, I shall see God, and where God him-self is the sensible acknowledged life of souls. *Miscel. Thoughts.*

ACADEMICAL DISPUTES APT TO PREJUDICE THE MINDS OF STUDENTS

It is exceeding hard to dispute without gaining some invisible

---

1 John 14:9.

prejudice and good liking to the opinion we defend. So devoted are we to ourselves, in this dark and degenerate state, that self-love too easily engages our favor to the cause we have espoused, and for no other reason than because we espoused it. Though we had no kindness before for an opinion that we maintain for disputing sake, yet if a plausible and smiling argument for it occurs in our hasty thoughts, how prone are we to hug the creature of our brain, and be almost in love with the opinion for the sake of the argument? I confess there are no such formal reasonings in our minds as these; yet we are insensibly captivated to esteem any thing that proceeds from ourselves: our passion first thinks it pity that such a happy argument of our own invention should be on the false side, and by secret insinuation, persuades the judgment to vote it true. How often have I experienced these fallacies working within me in verbal disputations before my tutor? And, for this reason, I have no great esteem of the method of our academical disputes, where the young sophisters are obliged to oppose the truth by the best arguments they can find, and the tutor defends it and assists the respondent. There is a certain wantonness of wit in youth, and a pleasing ambition of victory, which works in a young warm spirit, much stronger than a desire of truth. There is a strange delight in baffling the respondent, and it grows bigger sensibly, if we can put the president to a puzzle or a stand. The argument which is so successful, relishes better on the lips of the young opponent, and he begins to think that it is solid and unanswerable: "Surely my tutor's opinion can hardly be true; and though I thought I was put on the defense of a false doctrine, yet since I have found so good an argument for it, I can hardly believe it false." Then his invention works on to strengthen his suspicion, and at last he firmly believes the opinion he sought for. Often have I been in danger of such delusions as these, and feel myself too ready to submit to them now. Even a closet, and retirement, and our coolest meditations, are liable to these secret sophistries. Upon the first sight of an objection against our arguments, our thoughts are strangely hurried away to ransack the brain for a reply, and we torture our invention to make our side have the last word, before we call in cool judgment calmly to decide the difference; and thus from a hot defense of our own reasonings, we unimaginably slide into a cordial defense of the cause. *Miscel. Thoughts.*

CHRISTIAN REVELATION SUPERIOR TO HUMAN REASON

The Christian revelation has a vast preference above the mere principle of human reason, in that its motives are more numerous and powerful beyond all comparison. And if the motives to religion, which our reasoning powers can propose, may be called sufficient to equal, or rather to exceed all temptations to vice and impiety, because in the balance of reason they are more weighty, then the principles and motives of Christianity must be more abundantly sufficient, because, with an infinite superabundance, they outweigh all the temptations of flesh and sin, when put into the same balance of reason.

And on the other hand, if the motives of the gospel, numerous and powerful as they are, prove ineffectual to many thousands that hear them, surely the motives of mere reason, which are much fewer and feebler, are very insufficient in comparison with those of revelation. *Strength and Weakness of Human Reason.*

REASON ALONE NOT SUFFICIENT TO PROCURE TO MANKIND WISDOM AND BLESSEDNESS

If reason has only such a remote and speculative sufficiency, to guide and conduct mankind to happiness in a way of religion, if there are so very few (if any) who were never guided and conducted by it alone to happiness, then there is a most evident necessity of brighter light, clearer discoveries of duty, stronger motives and assistances, superior to what reason can furnish us with, to make mankind truly wise and blessed; and this light, and these motives, and assistances, are eminently to be found in the religion of Christ. *Strength and Weakness of Human Reason.*

DECENCY

That is decent, which is agreeable to our state, condition, or circumstances, whether it be in behavior, discourse, or action. *Logic.*

GRADUAL PROGRESS OF THE GOSPEL

This gospel was not revealed at once in its full glory to mankind. There have been several editions of it, or gradual discoveries of this grace, in all the former ages of the world.

As soon as ever Adam had sinned, and ruined himself and his posterity too, by laying the foundation of their sin and misery, it pleased God to publish this gospel by the promise of a Saviour, when he told our mother Eve, that *her seed should bruise the head of the serpent* that had deceived her.[1] This, by our divines, is generally called the first gospel; for, in the modern language of the New Testament, it signifies, that *Jesus Christ should come into this world to destroy the works of the devil.*[2]

Doubtless Noah, the second father of mankind, had some farther discoveries made to him, when the rainbow was appointed as the seal of a gracious covenant betwixt God and man; for the very promise of the continuance of the comfortable seasons of the year, being given to man in a way of mercy, do imply that God would not be irreconcilable to his fallen creatures. Nor can we reasonably suppose but that Adam and Noah, and all those most ancient patriarchs, had larger explications and comments of the first promise given them than Moses has recorded.

The gospel was renewed by revelations made to Abraham, when the Messiah, the Saviour, was promised to spring out of his family: *In thy seed shall all nations of the earth be blessed.*[3] Which promise is expressly called the gospel. There was also a type or pattern of our justification by faith in the way of the gospel, when *Abraham believed God* in his promises, etc. *it was*

---

1 Genesis 3:15.
2 1 John 3:8.
3 Galatians 3:8.

imputed to him for righteousness.[1]

Moses had a much larger discovery of the grace and mercy of God toward sinful man made to him, and to the Jews by him, than all the patriarchs put together: and this was not only done in the types, and figures, and ceremonies; not only in altars, sacrifices, washings, sprinklings, purifications, and in their redemption from Egypt, their miraculous salvations in the wilderness, and their safe conduct to Canaan, the land of promised rest; but he had many literal and express revelations of pardoning and sanctifying grace, which are scattered up and down in the five books which he wrote, and which he gave to the children of Israel to direct their religion. This is also called the gospel. *To them was the gospel preached as well as unto us,*[2] as those words ought to be translated. This same gospel was afterwards confirmed, illustrated, and enlarged by the succeeding prophets in the several ages of the Jewish church.

But *God, who at sundry times and in divers manners spoke* this gospel *to our fathers by the prophets, has in these latter days* published the same to us in a brighter manner, *by his Son Jesus*, the promised Saviour.[3] And since the death and resurrection of Christ, the apostles being sent by their exalted Lord, have given yet plainer and fuller declarations of this gospel to the children of men.

And upon this account it is several times called the gospel of Christ, not only because the offices and grace of Christ run through the whole of it, but also because the clearest discoveries of it are made to the world by Christ, and by his messengers the apostles.

Now from this last and fullest revelation of it in the New Testament, we may derive a fuller and more perfect knowledge of the gospel than all the former ages could attain. Hereby we learn that the gospel is a "promise of salvation from sin and hell by the death, righteousness, and grace of our Lord Jesus Christ to every one that is sincerely willing to accept of it by coming to Christ, or

---

1 Romans 4:22.

2 Hebrews 4:2.

3 Hebrews 1:1, 2.

trusting in him"; and it includes, also, "the promised aid of the Holy
Spirit to those who seek it, to enable them to receive this salvation,
and to fit them for the final possession of the promised glory." It
includes, also, "the revelation of the future resurrection, and last
judgment, and eternal life." To this end did the "Son of God come
into the world, that whosoever believes on him, should not perish,
but have eternal life."[1] *Orthodoxy and Christianity.*

THE GREAT DESIGN OF OUR SAVIOUR'S MINISTRY

The great design of our Saviour in his public appearance and
ministry upon earth, was to prove himself to wear the true characters of the Messiah, to deliver the Jews from many false expositions
and glosses which the Scribes and Pharisees of that day had given
to several parts of Scripture, to lead the world to a conviction of
their sins, and thereby prepare them to receive the doctrine of salvation with more zeal and desire; whereas the salvation itself, and the
manner whereby it was accomplished, was but briefly mentioned in
some few texts, and the rest was left to be explained by his apostles.
Orthodoxy and Christianity.

ADVICE WITH RESPECT TO PREACHING THE GOSPEL

Some may think it the duty and business of the day to tem-
porize, and by preaching the gospel a little more conformably to
natural religion, in a mere rational or legal form, to bring it down as
near as may be to their scheme, that we may gain them to hear and
approve it, or at least that we may not offend them. But I am rather
of opinion, that we should in such a day stand up for the defense of
the gospel in the full glory of its most important doctrines, and in
the full freedom of its grace; that we should preach it in its divinest
and most evangelical form, that the cross of Christ, by the promised
power of the Spirit, may vanquish the vain reasonings of men, and
that this despised doctrine, triumphing in the conversion of souls,
may confound the wise and the mighty, and silence the disputers of
this world. This was the bold and glorious method St. Paul took at

1 John 3:16.

Corinth, where learning, and reason, and philosophy flourished in pride; but they yielded several trophies of victory to the preaching of the cross. Paul could use the *wisdom of words* whenever he had occasion for it, and had the *excellency of speech* at command when he pleased; this appears in several parts of his writings; yet in his sermons at Corinth, he disclaimed it all, and *determined to know nothing among them but Christ, and him crucified.*[1] *Orthodoxy and Christianity.*

ORTHODOXY AND CHRISTIANITY

Let our conversation be such, as becomes the gospel in every form of it, whether absolute or conditional. Let our close walking with God be exemplary and instructive, that men may see our religion as well as hear it, and all may confess that while we preach the gospel, we are zealous observers of the law. Let us maintain upon our own hearts a sweet and honorable sense of the riches of free grace in Christ, together with a tender sense of the evil of sin, and a lively delight in holiness, that the daily experience of our own souls, and our inward Christianity which is taught us, and wrought in us by the Spirit of God, may instruct us how to preach to others. *Orthodoxy and Christianity.*

THE EXPEDIENCY OF ENGAGING THE AFFECTIONS
OF THE LOWER CLASSES OF MANKIND

God designed us to dwell here in such a wretched world, and I grant it is no small part of our state of trial: but to alleviate our unhappiness, he has mingled in the mass of mankind, some finer veins, some more intellectual and unprejudiced spirits, in whose conversation we may find suitable delight, and pleasures worthy of the rational nature. Why should not we suppose there are many other minds as happily turned as our own, and of superior size and more divine temper? All men have not been blessed with our advantages, yet their native felicity of thought may transcend ours. And as

---

1 1 Corinthians 2:2.

for the rest, God has ordained it our duty to associate with them for valuable ends and purposes in his providence, which regard both them and us. It is our business to endeavor to persuade them to lay aside their mistaken notions, to remove all the biases of error from their judgment, to quench their indignation against men of different opinions, and to enlarge their narrow souls, though we find it a difficult work. I have often seen what you complain of, and have been ready to conclude that when we have to do with vulgar souls, we should not lavish away our labor to convince them of innocent mistakes in matters of small importance, but only lay out our thoughts to rectify their notions in things that regard their present or future welfare. And when we reflect, how very impotent and low are the capacities of some ignorant creatures that we have to do with, how short their reasonings, how few their advantages to improve their minds, how incapable their judgments are of growing up to a solid and mature state by our utmost cultivation, and how unable their minds are in many cases, to discern and distinguish truth; I have been tempted to persuade myself, it is not dishonest policy to engage their affections a little. I know well that the passions were never made to judge of truth; but if we find persons who will never judge by any other rule, I would make inquiry whether we might not in some cases honestly make use of this. If we find that affection is the great gate of entrance into the judgments of the multitude, and reason is but like the back-door, or some meaner avenue, and seldom opened to let in any doctrine; may we not thence infer, that the softer arts of winning upon men, are to be studied by us as well as hard arguments. *Miscel. Thoughts.*

LIBERTY OF PRAYER

Indeed in the use of forms, there is no need of binding ourselves to a whole page together, as it stands in the book. In the name of God, let us stand fast in our Christian liberty, and maintain a just freedom of soul in our addresses to heaven; let us change, enlarge, or contract; let us add or omit, according to our peculiar sentiments, or our present frame of spirit. Mr. Jenks, a pious divine of the Church of England, has written an excellent treatise of the liberty of prayer, which I dare recommend to every sort of reader. But when we find the temper, the wants and the wishes of our hearts so happily expressed in the words of the composer, as that we know not how to frame other words so suitable, and so expressive of our own present state and case, why should we not address our God and our Saviour in this borrowed language? I confess, indeed, when long custom has induced a sort of flatness into these sounds, how happily soever the words might be at first chosen, then perhaps we shall want something new and various to keep nature awake to the devotion. Or, if we still confine ourselves to the forms we read, and forbid our spirits to exert their own pious sentiments we turn these engines of holy elevation into clogs and fetters. But when Christians make a prudent use of them, they have frequently experienced unknown advantage and delight. A dull and heavy hour in the closet has been relieved by the use of such devout composures of mingled meditation and prayer; and many a dry and barren heart has been enabled to offer up the first fruits of a sweet sacrifice to God, in the words of another man. The fire of devotion has been kindled by the help of some serious and pathetic forms, and the spirit of the worshiper, which has been straitened and bound up in itself, has found a blessed release by the pen of some pious writer. The wings of the soul have been first expanded toward God and heaven by some happy turn of fervent and holy language; she has been lifted up by this assistance above the earth and mortality; then she has given herself a more unconfined and various flight in the upper regions, she has traversed the heavenly world, she has felt herself within the circle of divine attraction, and has dwelt an hour with God. *Miscel. Thoughts.*

RULE FOR THE IMPROVEMENT OF THE REASONING FACULTIES

Accustom yourselves to clear and distinct ideas, to evident

propositions, to strong and convincing arguments. Converse much with those men and those books, and those parts of learning where you meet with the greatest clearness of thought, and force of reasoning. The mathematical sciences, and particularly arithmetic, geometry, and mechanics, abound with these advantages: and if there were nothing valuable in them for the uses of human life, yet the very speculative parts of this sort of learning are well worth our study; for by perpetual examples they teach us to conceive with clearness, to connect our ideas and propositions in a train of dependence, to reason with strength and demonstration, and to distinguish between truth and falsehood. Something of these sciences should be studied by every man who pretends to learning, and *that*, as Mr. Locke expresses it, "not so much to make us mathematicians, as to make us reasonable creatures."

We should gain such a familiarity with evidence of perception, and force of reasoning, and get such a habit of discerning clear truths, that the mind may be soon offended with obscurity and confusion: then we shall, as it were, naturally and with ease restrain our minds from rash judgment, before we attain just evidence of the proposition which is offered to us; and we shall with the same ease, and, as it were, naturally seize and embrace every truth that is proposed with just evidence.

This habit of conceiving clearly, of judging justly, and of reasoning well, is not to be obtained merely by the happiness of constitution, the brightness of genius, the best natural parts, or the best collection of logical precepts: it is custom and practice that must form this habit. We must apply ourselves to it till we perform all this readily, and without reflecting on rules. A coherent thinker, and a strict reasoner, is not to be made at once by a set of rules, any more than a good painter or musician may be formed extempore, by an excellent lecture on music or painting. It is of infinite importance therefore in our younger years to be taught both the value and the practice of conceiving clearly and of reasoning right; for when we are grown up to the middle of life, or past it, it is no wonder we should not learn good reasoning, any more than that an ignorant clown should not be able to learn fine language, dancing, or courtly behavior, when his rustic airs have grown up with him till the age of forty.

For want of this care, some persons of rank and education dwell all their days among obscure ideas; they conceive and judge always in confusion, they take weak arguments for demonstration, they are led away with the disguises and shadows of truth. Now if such persons happen to have a bright imagination, a volubility of speech, and copiousness of language, they not only impose many errors upon their own understandings, but they stamp the image of their own mistakes upon their neighbors also, and spread their errors abroad. *Logic.*

ADVICE ON THE SUBJECT OF ARGUMENT

Be not so solicitous about the number as the weight of your arguments, especially in proving any proposition that admits of natural certainly or of complete demonstration. Many times we do injury to a cause by dwelling upon trifling arguments. We amuse our hearers with uncertainties, by multiplying the number of feeble reasonings, before we mention those which are more substantial, conclusive, and convincing. And too often we yield up our own assent to mere probable arguments, where certain proofs may be obtained. *Logic.*

Labor in all your arguings to enlighten the understanding, as well as to conquer and captivate the judgment. Argue in such a manner as may give a natural, distinct, and solid knowledge of things to your hearers, as well as to force their assent by a mere proof of the question. *Logic.*

EXCELLENT USE OF SIMILITUDES

Similitudes and allusions have oftentimes a very happy influence to explain some difficult truth, and to render the idea of it familiar and easy. Where the resemblance is just and accurate, the influence of a simile may proceed so far as to show the possibility of the thing in question: but similitudes must not be taken as a solid proof of the truth or existence of those things to which they have a resemblance.

A too great deference paid to similitudes, or an utter rejection of them, seem to be too extremes, and ought to be avoided. The late ingenious Mr. Locke, even in his inquiries after truth, makes a great use of similes for frequent illustration, and is very happy in the invention of them, though he warns us also lest we mistake them for conclusive arguments.

Yet let it be noted here, that a parable, or a similitude used by any author, may give a sufficient proof of the true sense and meaning of that author, provided that he draw not his similitude beyond the scope and design for which it was brought; as when our Saviour affirms, *I will come unto thee as a thief;*[1] this will plainly prove that he ascribes the *unexpectedness* of his appearance, though it is by no means to be drawn to signify any *injustice* in his design. *Logic.*

ENTRANCE UPON THE WORLD

Curino was a young man brought up to a respectable trade; the term of his apprenticeship was almost expired, and he was contriving how he might venture into the world with safety, and pursue business with innocence and success. Among his near kindred, Serenus was one, a gentleman of considerable character in the sacred profession; and after he had consulted with his father, who was a merchant of great esteem and experience, he also thought fit to seek a word of advice from the divine. Serenus had such a respect for his young kinsman, that he set his thought at work on this subject, and with some tender expressions, which melted the youth into tears, he put into his hand a paper of his best counsels. Curino entered upon business, pursued his employment with uncommon advantage, and under the blessing of heaven advanced himself to a considerable estate. He lived with honor in the world, and gave a luster to the religion he professed; and after a long life of piety and usefulness, he died with a sacred composure of soul, under the influence of the Christian hope. Some of his neighbors wondered at his felicity in this world, joined with so much innocence, and such severe virtue.

---

1 Revelation 3:3.

But after his death this paper was found in his closet, which was drawn up by his kinsman in holy orders, and was supposed to have a large share in procuring his happiness.

ADVICE TO A YOUNG MAN

I. Kinsman, I presume you desire to be happy here, and hereafter; you know there are a thousand difficulties which attend this pursuit; some of them perhaps you foresee, but there are multitudes which you could never think of. Never trust therefore to your own understanding in the things of this world, where you can have the advice of a wise and faithful friend; nor dare venture the more important concerns of your soul, and your eternal interests in the world to come, upon the mere light of nature, and the dictates of your own reason; since the Word of God, and the advice of heaven, lies in your hands. Vain and thoughtless indeed are those children of pride, who choose to turn heathens in the midst of Great Britain; who live upon the mere religion of nature and their own stock, when they have been trained up among all the superior advantages of Christianity, and the blessings of divine revelation and grace.

II. Whatsoever your circumstances may be in this world, still value your Bible as your best treasure; and whatsoever be your employment here, still look upon religion as your best business. Your Bible contains eternal life in it, and all the riches of the upper world; and religion is the only way to become a possessor of them.

III. To direct your carriage towards God, converse particularly with the book of Psalms: David was a man of sincere and eminent devotion. To behave aright among men, acquaint yourself with the whole book of Proverbs: Solomon was a man of large experience and wisdom. And to perfect your directions in both those, read the gospels and the epistles; you will find the best of rules and the best of examples there, and those more immediately suited to the Christian life.

IV. As a man, maintain strict temperance and sobriety, by a wise government of your appetites and passions. As a neighbor, influence and engage all around you to be your friends, by a temper and carriage made up of prudence and goodness; and let the poor have a certain share in all your yearly profits. As a trader, keep that golden sentence of our Saviour's ever before you, *Whatsoever you would that men should do unto you, do you also unto them.*[1]

V. While you make the precepts of Scripture the constant rule of your duty, you may with courage rest upon the promises of Scripture as the springs of your encouragement. All divine assistances and divine recompenses are contained in them. The spirit of light and grace is promised to assist them that ask it. Heaven and glory are promised to reward the faithful and the obedient.

VI. In every affair of life, begin with God. Consult him in every thing that concerns you. View him as the author of all your blessings and all your hopes, as your best friend and your eternal portion. Meditate on him in this view, with a continual renewal of your trust in him, and a daily surrender of yourself to him, till you feel that you love him most entirely, that you serve him with sincere delight, and that you cannot live a day without God in the world.

VII. You know yourself to be a man, an indigent creature, and a sinner, and you profess to be a Christian, a disciple of the blessed Jesus: but never think you know Christ nor yourself as you ought, till you find a daily need of him for righteousness and strength, for pardon and sanctification; and let him be your constant introducer to the great God, though he sits upon a throne of grace. Remember his own words, *No man cometh to the Father but by me.*[2]

VIII. Make prayer a pleasure and not a task, and then you will not forgot nor omit it. If ever you have lived in a praying family, never let it be your fault if you do not live in one always. Believe that day, that hour, or those minutes, to be all wasted and lost, which any worldly pretences would tempt you to save out of the public worship of the church, the certain and constant duties of the closet, or any

1 Matthew 7:12.
2 John 14:6.

necessary services for God and godliness. Beware lest a blast attend it, and not a blessing. If God had not reserved one day in seven to himself, I fear religion would have been lost out of the world; and every day of the week is exposed to a curse, which has no morning religion.

IX. See that you watch and labor, as well as pray. Diligence and dependence must be united in the practice of every Christian. It is the same wise man acquaints us, that the hand of the diligent, and the blessing of the Lord, join together to make us rich,[1] rich in the treasures of body or mind, of time or eternity.

It is your duty indeed, under a sense of your own weakness, to pray daily against sin; but if you would effectually avoid it, you must also avoid temptation, and every dangerous opportunity. Set a double guard wheresoever you feel or suspect any enemy at hand. The world without, and the heart within, have so much flattery and deceit in them, that we must keep a sharp eye upon both, lest we are trapped into mischief between them.

X. Honor, profit, and pleasure, have been sometimes called the world's trinity, they are its three chief idols; each of them is sufficient to draw a soul off from God, and ruin it for ever. Beware of them, therefore, and of all their subtle insinuations, if you would be innocent or happy.

Remember that the honor which comes from God, the approbation of heaven, and of your own conscience, are infinitely more valuable than all the esteem or applause of men. Dare not venture one step out of the road of heaven, for fear of being laughed at for walking strictly in it. It is a poor religion that cannot stand against a jest.

Sell not your hopes of heavenly treasures, nor any thing that belongs to your eternal interest, for any of the advantages of the present life: *What shall it profit a man to gain the whole world, and lose his own soul?*[2]

Remember also the words of the wise man: *He that loveth*

1 Proverbs 10:4, 22.
2 Mark 8:36.

pleasure shall be a poor man, he that indulges himself in *wine and oil*, that is in drinking, in feasting, and in sensual gratifications, *shall not be rich*.[1] It is one of St. Paul's characters of a most degenerate age, when *men become lovers of pleasure, more than lovers of God*.[2] And that *fleshly lusts war against the soul*,[3] is St. Peter's caveat to the Christians of his time.

XI. Preserve your conscience always soft and sensible. If but one sin force its way into that tender part of the soul, and dwell easy there, the road is paved for a thousand iniquities.

And take heed that under any scruple, doubt, or temptation whatsoever, you never let any reasonings satisfy your conscience, which will not be a sufficient answer or apology to the great Judge at the last day.

XII. Keep this thought ever in your mind: It is a world of vanity and vexation in which you live; the flatteries and promises of it are vain and deceitful; prepare, therefore, to meet disappointments. Many of its occurrences are teasing and vexatious. In every ruffling storm without, possess your spirit in patience, and let all becalm and serene within. Clouds end tempests are only found in the lower skies; the heavens above are ever bright and clear. Let your heart and hope dwell much in these serene regions; live as a stranger here on earth, but as a citizen of heaven, if you will maintain a soul at ease.

XIII. Since in many things we offend all, and there is not a day passes which is perfectly free from sin, let *repentance towards God and faith in our Lord Jesus Christ*, be your daily work. A frequent renewal of those exercises which make a Christian at first, will be a constant evidence of your sincere Christianity, and give you peace in life, and hope in death.

XIV. Ever carry about with you such a sense of the uncertainty of every thing in this life, and of life itself, as to put nothing off

1 Proverbs 21:17.
2 2 Timothy 3:4.
3 1 Peter 2:11.

till tomorrow, which you can conveniently do today. Dilatory persons are frequently opposed to surprise and hurry in everything that belongs to them; the time is come and they are unprepared. Let the concerns of your soul and your shop, your trade and your religion, lie always in such order, as far as possible, that death, at a short warning, may be no occasion of a disquieting tumult in your spirit, and that you may escape the anguish of a bitter repentance in a dying hour. Farewell.

Phronimus, a considerable East-land merchant, happened upon a copy of these advices about the time when he permitted his son to commence a partnership with him in his trade; he transcribed them with his own hand, and made a present of them to the youth, together with the articles of partnership. "Here, young man," said he, "is a paper of more worth than these articles. Read it over once a month, till it is wrought in your very soul and temper. Walk by these rules, and I can trust my estate in your hands. Copy out these counsels in your life, and you will make me and yourself easy and happy." *Miscel. Thoughts.*

AGAINST INDULGING THE ANGRY PASSIONS

Take care of giving up the reins entirely to an angry passion, though it pretend sin for its object, lest it run to an ungovernable excess. It is St. Paul's counsel, *Be angry, and sin not,*[1] so hard it is to be angry upon my account without sinning. It was a happy comparison, (whosoever first invented it) that the passions of our Saviour were like pure water in a clear glass; shake it never so much, and it is pure still; there was no defilement in his holy soul by the warmest agitation of all those powers of his animal nature; but ours are like water with mud at the bottom, and we can scarce shake the glass with the gentlest motion, but the mud arises, and diffuses itself abroad, polluting both the water and the vessel. Our irascible passions can scarce be indulged a moment, but they are ready to defile the whole man. *Miscel. Thoughts.*

---

1 Ephesians 4:26.

Where the mere *appearance* of an angry passion will attain the same end, I would not choose to give myself the trouble and inquietude of feeling a *real* one. Why should I suffer my blood and spirits to rise into disorder, if the picture of anger in my countenance, and the sound of it imitated in my voice, will effectually discourage and reprove the vice I would forbid? If I am but wise enough to raise the appearance of resentment, I need not be at the pains to throw myself into this uneasy ferment. Is it not better for me, as a man and a Christian, to maintain a calm sedate aversion to sin, and express my dislike of it, sometimes, at least, rather by a counterfeit than real anger. If hypocrisy be lawful any where, surely it may be allowed in this case to dissemble. *Miscel. Thoughts.*

THE REASON OF OUR SAVIOUR SPEAKING IN PARABLES

Since these expressions of our Saviour concerning *eating his flesh and drinking his blood*, sound very harsh and absurd in the literal sense of them, we must then seek out the plainest and truest figurative sense: now this is very near at hand, and might be obvious to those among them who had read the Jewish prophets with care. When he tells them that the *living bread is his flesh, which he gives for the life of the world*,[1] it gives an intimation that his flesh or body was to be broken or die as a proper sacrifice of atonement for our guilt, which deserved death, which was not proper to be spoken too publicly and plainly in his lifetime; and further, that his blood was to be shed for the remission of our sins, and to procure life for us; and that we must not only receive his doctrine, but we must trust in him for our remission, and feed upon this sacrifice by faith, as the Jews eat part of their sacrifices; and that we must live upon it by trusting therein. And since the Messiah was foretold to be made an offering for sin by the prophets, and since feeding upon sin-offerings was common to the Jewish religion,[2] the thoughtful

1 John 6:51.
2 Leviticus 6:25, 26.

hearers might arrive at something of the sense and meaning of our Saviour's meaning in this figurative language.

But suppose the Jews, when he first spoke it, could not well understand him; consider they had abused his person, and derided his doctrine, and having so far rejected the light, they deserved to be left in darkness, amidst figures and parables, as Christ himself declares.[1]

I add yet further, there are several things which Christ in his lifetime spoke in prophetic or parabolical language, for this reason, as I before hinted, that they were not fit and proper to be spoken too plainly at that season; but he left the expressions to be explained by the events. The death of Christ, which was not far off, and the ministry of the apostles quickly afterward representing his death as a propitiation for our sins, gave us a plain clue to lead us into the sense of Christ in these figurative and prophetic speeches, all which are so happily accommodable to these ideas and doctrines of Christ's atonement for sin, and our faith therein, as gives much satisfaction to the thinking reader, that they were designed and intended hereby. *Redeemer and Sanctifier.*

ON THE SACRIFICE OF OUR BLESSED REDEEMER

To me it is evident as the sunbeams, that while the New Testament restores natural religion to us in the brightest and fairest light, and lays the strongest obligations on us to perform all the duties of it; yet it still supposes the impossibility of our salvation thereby, through our own incapacity to perform these duties perfectly; and therefore it sets forth to our view the blessed sacrifice of the Son of God, which is the only true and proper sacrifice for our sins. Nor does it set this atonement in the room of our endeavors after inward religion and real virtue, but in the room of all other sacrifices whatsoever, whether Jewish or Gentile. As for all the Jewish offerings, they were but appointed types of the sacrifice of Christ, and could never really atone for the sins of mankind against God as ruler of the world. And the sacrifices of the Gentiles, what were they, but substitutions and offerings of

---

1 Mark 4:12.

beasts or men upon their altars, such as God never appointed, and therefore would never accept, either as real atonements, or as figures of the true propitiation and atonement. This is the very evident sense of St. Paul, in Romans 8:13. *There is no condemnation of them that are in Jesus Christ, i.e.* who trust in him as the medium of their pardon, and *who walk not after the flesh, but after the spirit, i.e.* who live holy lives: *What the law could not do in that it was weak,* and unable to justify us though *the flesh, i.e.* through our inability to perform it, God has done this by *sending his own Son in the likeness of sinful flesh, and a sacrifice for sin,* (as it is in the Greek) *has condemned in the flesh,* etc. and thus made a way through his sacrifice of atonement for our justification and sanctification.

But lest the force and significancy of any of these Scriptures should be lost for want of a true idea of what I mean by a "proper and complete atonement made for the sins of men," I would here give some general explication of what I intend by the word. I do not pretend to such accuracy and exactness of definition, as might be expected from a civilian, or a divine;[1] but I would speak what I take to be the common sense of the thinking part of mankind in this matter and more particularly the sense of the writers of the Old and New Testaments.

By atonement for sin, therefore, I do not mean any such thing as shall, in a proper and literal sense, appease the wrath of God, the offended Governor, which is supposed to be kindled against his sinful creatures, and shall incline his heart to mercy, which was before determined upon vengeance; for though this doctrine may be represented sometimes after the manner of men, yet this is an idea or supposition, in many respects, inconsistent with the attributes and actions of the blessed God, and with the doctrine of the New Testament. In that book God represents himself as *rich in mercy,* and for this reason he pitied sinful creatures, who had broken his

---

1 The author does not speak here in his own character of a clergyman: in the preface to the work from which this extract is made, he says, "Let it be remembered that this book is but a sort of conversation-piece among a few private friends, who pretend not to theological accuracies."

law, and had deserved to die, before he had received any atonement; and therefore God himself provided, and sent his own Son
to become a sacrifice and atonement, and a ransom for them; he
appointed him to be a surety for us, the *just for the unjust*, and to
suffer death in the room and stead of sinners.

By the words atonement or propitiation, I mean therefore, some
toilsome and painful thing to be done or suffered, or both, by Jesus
Christ, the Son of God, in the room and stead of sinful men, as a
penance or punishment on the account of their sins; and this by the
wise and righteous appointment of God the universal Governor,
shall excuse the penitent offender from the punishment that was
due, and obtain his pardon, because it shall give a recompense to the
authority of the divine lawgiver for the affront which was put upon
him by the sins of men, and shall make some reparation of honor
to his holy law which was broken. And this is not only intended to
manifest the evil nature and the desert of sin, together with God's
hatred of it; but it shall also answer the demand and design of the
threatening by such actual pain or punishment, though it is laid on
the surety instead of the offender; and thus it may secure the law
from being wilfully broken, in time to come, as effectually as if the
offenders themselves had been punished. Such a pain, penance, or
punishment, are the humiliation and sufferings of Jesus Christ, his
labors and sorrows: and it is in this sense that the language of expiation or atonement, of propitiation and ransom, is so often used.[1]
It is in this sense that he was said to become a "sacrifice for us, to
bear our sins on his own body on the tree," and "to be made sin," or
"a sin offering for us, who knew no sin" himself: in this sense he is
said to be "made a curse, and suffer death for us," and to redeem us
from it thereby, because the law curses every sinner, and pronounces
death upon him. Now by these appointed sufferings of the Son of

---

1 Christ, after he became our surety, was not, nor could be delivered from
those sorrows which were the punishment of our sins, he being as our
expiatory sacrifice, not only on the occasion of our sins, but in our stead,
to bear the punishment of our iniquity. Whitby on Hebrews 5:3.

God, in the room and stead of sinful men, there is an honorable amends made to the Governor of the world for the violation of his law, and a glorious way made for the exercise of mercy in the pardon of the sinner; and that without any imputation or reflection upon the holiness of God's nature and conduct, or any suspicion of the justice of his government, as if he would connive at sin; since he discovers and declares, that in his passing by all the sins of his people in former ages, and in pardoning and in *justifying* sinners now *who believe in Christ*, he will manifest justice or righteousness by requiring such a sacrifice whereby sin shall be punished, though the sinner be spared. This is the plain meaning of the apostle, "Being justified freely by his grace, through the redemption that is in Jesus Christ, whom God hath set forth to be a propitiation through faith in his blood, to declare his righteousness for the remission of sins that are past, through the forbearance of God: to declare, I say, at this time his righteousness, that he might be just, and the justifier of him that believeth in Jesus":[1] which text our fathers have ever thought an unanswerable proof as well as a clear explication of this doctrine. And I think there is abundant reason in Scripture for us to support this sentiment of our fathers, though all the modern writers should agree to oppose it. *Redeemer and Sanctifier.*

CURIOSITY TO BE ENCOURAGED IN YOUNG PERSONS

Curiosity is a useful spring of knowledge: it should be encouraged in children, and awakened by frequent and familiar methods of talking with them. It should be indulged in youth, but not without a prudent moderation. In those who have too much, it should be limited by a wise and gentle restraint or delay, lest by wandering after every thing, they learn nothing to perfection. In those who have too little, it should be excited, lest they grow stupid, narrow spirited, self-satisfied, and never attain a treasure of ideas, or an aptitude of understanding. *Posthumous Works.*

---

1 Romans 3:24, 25, 26.

FAULT OF YOUNG PREACHERS REPROVED

Young preachers just come from the schools, are often tempted to fill their sermons with logical and metaphysical terms in explaining their text, and feed their hearers with sonorous words of vanity. This scholastic language, perhaps may flatter their own ambition, and raise a wonderment at their learning among the staring multitude, without any manner of influence towards the instruction of the ignorant, or the reformation of the immoral or impious: these terms of art are but the tools of an artificer, by which his work is wrought in private; but the tools ought not to appear in the finished workmanship. *Posthumous Works.*

GENTLENESS OF ADDRESS SUCCESSFUL IN CONVINCING OUR OPPONENTS

The softest and gentlest address to the erroneous, is the best way to convince them of their mistake. Sometimes it is necessary to represent to our opponent, that he is not far off from the truth, and that you would fain draw him a little nearer to it; commend and establish whatever he says that is just and true, as our blessed Saviour treated the young scribe, when he answered well concerning the two great commandments: "Thou art not far, says our Lord, from the kingdom of heaven."[1] Imitate the mildness and conduct of the blessed Jesus.

Come as near to your opponent as you can in all your propositions, and yield to him as much as you dare, in a consistence with truth and justice.

It is a very great and fatal mistake in persons who attempt to convince and reconcile others to their party, when they make the difference appear as wide as possible: this is shocking to any person who is to be convinced; he will choose rather to keep and maintain his own opinions, if he cannot come into yours without renouncing and abandoning every thing that he believed before. Human nature must be flattered a little as well as reasoned with, that so

1 Mark 12:34.

the argument may be able to come at his understanding, which otherwise will be thrust off at a distance. If you charge a man with nonsense and absurdities, with heresy and self-contradiction, you take a very wrong step towards convincing him.

Remember that error is not to be rooted out of the mind of man by reproaches and railings, by flashes of wit and biting jests, by loud exclamations or sharp ridicule: long declamations and triumph over our neighbor's mistake, will not prove the way to convince him; these are signs either of a bad cause, or of want of arguments or capacity for the defense of a good one. *Posthumous Works.*

THE PROGRESSIVE EXPIRATION OF PARENTAL AUTHORITY

It is hard to say, at what exact time of life, the child is exempted from the sovereignty of parental dictates. Perhaps it is much juster to suppose that this sovereignty diminishes by degrees as the child grows in understanding and capacity, and is more and more capable of exerting his own intellectual powers, than to limit this matter by months and years.

When childhood and youth are so far expired, that the reasoning faculties are grown up to any just measure of maturity, it is certain that persons ought to begin to inquire into the reasons of their own faith and practice in all the affairs of life and religion; but as reason does not arrive at this power and self-sufficiency in any single moment of time, so there is no single moment when a child should at once cast off all its former beliefs and practices; but by degrees, and in slow succession, he should examine them as opportunity and advantages offer; and either confirm, or doubt of, or change them, according to the leadings of conscience and reason, with all its best advantages of information. *Posthumous Works.*

IMPLICIT OBEDIENCE DUE TO DIVINE REVELATION

Where doctrines of divine revelation are plainly published, together with sufficient proofs of their revelation, all mankind are bound to receive them, though they cannot perfectly understand them; for we know that God is true, and cannot dictate falsehood. *Posthumous Works.*

ANCIENT ROUGHNESS AND MODERN REFINEMENT OF LANGUAGE CONTRASTED AND CENSURED

Some of our fathers neglected politeness perhaps too much, and indulged a coarseness of style, and a rough or awkward pronunciation; but we have such a value for elegancy, and so nice a taste for what we call polite, that we dare not spoil the cadence of a period to quote a text of Scripture in it, nor disturb the harmony of our sentences, to number or to name the heads of our discourse. And for this reason, I have heard it hinted, that the name of Christ has been banished out of polite sermons, because it is a monosyllable of so many consonants, and so harsh a sound. *Posthumous Works.*

ADVICE TO AUTHORS

As a writer or a speaker should not wander from his subject to fetch in foreign matter from afar, so neither should he amass together and drag in all that can be said, even on his appointed theme of discourse; but he should consider what is his chief design, what is the end he has in view, and then to make every part of his discourse subserve that design. If he keep his great end always in his eye, he will pass hastily over those parts or appendages of his subject which have no evident connection with his design; or he will entirely omit them, and hasten continually towards his intended mark; employing his time, his study, and his labor, chiefly on that part of his subject which is most necessary to attain his present and proper end. *Posthumous Works.*

When an author desires a friend to revise his work, it is too frequent a practice to disallow almost every correction which a judicious friend would make; he apologizes for this word, and the other expression; he vindicates this sentence, and gives his reasons for another paragraph, and scarce ever submits to a correction; and this utterly discourages the freedom that a true friend would take, in pointing out our mistakes. Such writers who are so full of themselves, may go on to admire their own incorrect performances, and expose their works and their follies to the world without pity. *Posthumous Works.*

If you have not the advantage of friends to survey your writings, then read them over yourself, and all the way consider what will be the sentence and judgment of all the various characters of mankind upon them: think what one of your own party would say, or what would be the sense of an adversary: imagine what a curious or a malicious man, what a captious or an envious critic, what a vulgar or a learned reader would object, either to the matter, the manner, or the style: and be sure and think with yourself, what you yourself could say against your own writing, if you were of a different opinion, or a stranger to the writer: and by these means you will obtain some hints, whereby to correct and improve your own work, and to guard it better against the censures of the public, as well as to render it more useful to that part of mankind for whom you chiefly design it. *Posthumous Works.*

METHOD OF STRENGTHENING THE MEMORY OF CHILDREN

I have known children, who from their early years have been constantly trained up and taught to remember a few sentences of a sermon besides the text, and by this means have grown up by decrees to know all the distinct parts and branches of a discourse, and in time to write down half the sermon after they came home, to their own consolation, and the improvement of their friends: whereas those who have been never taught to use their memories in their younger parts of life, lose every thing from their thoughts when it is past off from their ears, and come home from noble and edifying discourses, pleased, it may be, with the transient sound, and commending the preacher, but uninstructed, unimproved, without any growth in knowledge or piety. *Posthumous Works.*

RELIGIOUS AND MORAL DUTY TO BE ENCOURAGED IN CHILDREN

Conscience is another natural power of the soul, wherein the principles of virtue and rules of duty to God and man are to be laid up: it is something within us that calls us to account for our faults, and by which we pass a judgment concerning ourselves and our actions.

Children have a conscience within them, and it should be awakening early to its duty. They should be taught to reflect and look back upon their own behavior, and call themselves often to account, to compare their deeds with those good rules and principals laid up in their minds, and to see how far they have complied with them, and how far they have neglected them. Parents should teach their children to pay a religious respect to the inward dictates of virtue within them, to examine their actions continually by the light of their own consciences, and to rejoice when they can approve themselves to their own minds, that they have acted well according to the best of their knowledge: they ought also to attend to the inward reproofs of their own conscience, and mourn, and be ashamed, and repent, when they have sinned against their light. It is of admirable use toward all the practices of religion and every virtue, to have conscience well stored with good principles, and to be always kept tender and watchful; it is proper that children should learn to reverence and obey this inward monitor betimes, that every willful sin may give their consciences a sensible pain and uneasiness, and that they may be disposed to sacrifice every thing else to considerations of conscience, and to endure any extremities, rather than act contrary to it. *Posthumous Works.*

ILL CONSEQUENCES OF TERRIFYING YOUNG MINDS BY DISMAL NARRATIVES

Let not any persons that are near them terrify their tender minds with dismal stories of witches and ghosts, of devils and evil spirits, of fairies and bugbears in the dark. This has a most mischievous effect on some children, and has fixed in their constitutions such a rooted slavery and fear, that they have scarce dared to be left alone all their lives, especially in the night. These stories have made such a deep and frightful impression on their tender fancies, that it has enervated their souls, it has broken their spirits early, it has grown up with them, and mingled with their religion, it has laid a wretched foundation for melancholy and distracting sorrows. Let these sort of informations be reserved for their firmer years, and let them not be told in their hearing till they can judge what truth or reality there is in them, and be made sensible how much is owing to romance and fiction.

Nor let their little hearts be frighted at three or four years old, with shocking and bloody histories, with massacres and martyrdoms, with cuttings and burnings, with the images of horrible and barbarous murders, with racks and red hot pincers, with engines of torment and cruelty, with mangled limbs and carcasses drenched in gore. It is time enough, when their spirits are grown a little firmer, to acquaint them with these madnesses and miseries of human nature. There is no need that the history of the holy confessors and martyrs should be set before their thoughts so early, in all their most ghastly shapes and colors. These things, when they are older, may be of excellent use to discover to them the wicked and bloody principles of persecution, both among the heathens and papists; and to teach them the power of the grace of Christ, in supporting these poor sufferers under all the torments which they sustained for the love of God and the truth. *Posthumous Works.*

PARTICULAR PARTS OF THE BIBLE NOT TO BE READ BY CHILDREN

There should be a wise conduct in showing children what parts of the Bible they should read: for though the Word of God expresses all things with due decency, yet there are some things which have been found necessary to be spoken of in Scripture, both in the laws of Moses, and in the representation of the wickedness of the Gentiles in the New Testament, in which adult persons have been concerned, which there is no necessity for children to read or hear, and they may be passed over, or omitted among them. The Jews were wont to withhold Solomon's Song from their children till they were thirty years old: and the late pious and prudent bishop Tillotson, in a manuscript which I have seen, wishes that those parts of the Bible wherein there are some of the affairs of mankind expressed "too naturally," as he calls it, were omitted in the public lessons of the church: I think they may as well be excepted also out of the common lessons of children, and out of the daily course of reading in family worship. *Posthumous Works.*

RULES FOR MODERATING OUR ANGER

Our natures are so perverse and corrupt, that it is very hard for us to give a loose to any angry passion against men, without running into some sentiments of malice or revenge, and thereby sinning against God. Our anger is very apt to kindle about trifles, or upon mere suspicion, without just cause; or sometimes rises too high, where the cause may be just; or it continues too long, and turns into hatred: and in either of these three cases it becomes sinful.

It is therefore with the utmost caution that this passion should ever be suffered to arise: and unless we quickly suppress it again, we shall be in great danger of bringing guilt upon our souls. The blessed apostle therefore connects the permission, the caution, and the restraint together, "Be angry, and sin not: let not the sun go down upon your wrath."[1] *Doctrine of the Passions.*

Let your desires and aversions to the common objects and occurrences in this life be but few and feeble. Make it your daily business to moderate your aversions and desires, and to govern them by reason. This will guard you against many a ruffle of spirit, both of anger and sorrow. *Doctrine of the Passions.*

Suffer not your thoughts to dwell on the injuries you have received, or of the provoking words that have been spoken against you. Not only learn the art of neglecting injuries at the time you receive them, but let them grow less and less every moment, till they die out of your mind. Suffer not your musing imagination, when you are alone, to swell and magnify the provocations that have been given you, nor to blow up the fire of this uneasy passion.

---

1 Ephesians 4:26.

Avoid much conversation with men of wrath, and endeavor to keep clear of all disputes with weak minds, with obstinate spirits, and especially with persons of an angry and peevish temper, as far as you can. If the flint and steel strike against each other in a way of dispute, the sparks of fire will be ready to fly out, and the angry flame will be kindled.

Love your neighbor as yourself.[1] You are not immediately kindled into wrath against yourself, nor express it with such violence, though you have often done yourself more injury by your own sins than all other persons ever could do you. You do not bear malice against yourself, nor hate yourself, though you have, perhaps, some evil qualities belonging to you, and you have often sinned against your own soul: you forbear yourself long, and you forgive yourself easily: learn then to forbear and forgive your neighbors. *Doctrine of the Passions.*

Anger is a short madness; it throws a person off his guard; neither the truth nor reason appear to him as reason or truth: the violence of the passion throws off all restraints, the frenzy disdains all law and justice; and drives the man to wild extravagance. Is this the lovely, the desirable pattern that you choose to imitate? Do you like this figure so well as to put it on your self?

Live always under the eye of God, and suppress rising anger with the reverence of his name and presence. Remember that a holy God and holy angels behold you; and are you not ashamed to appear in their sight under all the extravagant disorders of this passion? Remember the dignity of your nature as a man, and your character as a Christian, and a child of God.

Keep the sacred example of Jesus ever before your eyes: how meek under the vilest affronts! how patient under the rudest injuries and most barbarous treatment! how forgiving, even to his bloody murderers! how did he return the highest good for the greatest evil! and paid down his blood and life to redeem his enemies from hell, and to purchase eternal joy and glory for them! Let such a mind be in you as was in Christ the Son of God, who being reviled, reviled

1 Mark 12:31.

not again; and when he suffered, he threatened not: leaving us an example that we should follow his steps. *Doctrine of the Passions.*

It is said concerning Julius Caesar, that upon any provocation, he would repeat the Roman alphabet, before he suffered himself to speak, that he might be more just and calm in his resentments. The delay of a few moments has set many seeming affronts in a juster and kinder light; it has often lessened, if not annihilated, the supposed injury, and prevented violence and revenge. *Doctrine of the Passions.*

Think with yourself, how much injury you do yourself, by suffering your angry passions to rise and prevail. The fire of wrath and resentment preys upon your nature, destroys your health and ease, fills your spirit with tumults and disquietudes, exposes you to shame before men, breaks the peace of your conscience, brings you under guilt before God, and makes a painful preparation for bitter repentance. Why will you punish yourself because another has injured you? or, if another man be rude and wrathful, ill-natured and ill-bred, why will you imitate him, and expose yourself?

Think again, how much more pleasure and glory there is in overcoming the violence of your own spirit, than in yielding to your headstrong passions, and suffering yourselves to be carried away with the torrent of your own resentments. *He that rules his own spirit, is a greater hero than he that conquers a city.*[1]

To be angry about trifles, is mean and childish; to rage and be furious, is brutish; and to maintain perpetual wrath, is akin to the practice and temper of devils: but to prevent or suppress rising resentment, is wise and glorious, is manly and divine.

This one piece of conduct will raise our reputation for wisdom among men, more than a hundred fine speeches, or superior airs; and will greatly adorn our characters as persons of piety. *The wisdom that is from above is peaceable, gentle, and easy to be intreated.*[2] *Doctrine of the Passions.*

Think with yourself how many greater crimes has the blessed

1 Proverbs 16:32.
2 James 3:17.

God forgiven you, if you are a Christian indeed; and will you not forgive your brother his petty offenses? Has the Maker and Lord of heaven and earth forgiven you ten thousand talents, and will you not forgive your brother a hundred pence? Did the Son of God make himself a sacrifice for your offenses, that you might be pardoned, and will you make your brother, who has offended you, a sacrifice to your fury?

But consider farther, that if you do not forgive your brother, who has offended you, you cannot expect to be forgiven of God: nay, it is evident, according to the express sentence of the gospel, you cannot be forgiven without it. "If you forgive not men their trespasses, neither will your heavenly Father forgive you." Do you not pray for pardon of your trespasses, even as you forgive those who trespass against you, and will you sin against your own prayers? *Doctrine of the Passions.*

AGAINST INDULGING IMPROPER CURIOSITY

Restrain your needless curiosity, and all solicitous inquiries into things which were better unknown. How many plentiful springs of fear, sorrow, anger, and hatred, have been found out and broken up by this laborious digging? Have a care of an over-curious search into such things as might have safely remained for ever secret, and the ignorance of them had prevented many foolish and hurtful passions. A fond solicitude to know all that our friends or our foes say of us is often recompensed with vexing disquietudes and anguish of soul. *Doctrine of the Passions.*

HABITUAL REFLECTING UPON DEATH RECOMMENDED

Live much in the expectation of death, and in the view and hope of eternal things. Death and judgment, heaven and hell, are such grand and awful ideas, that where they are duly considered, they will make the things of this life appear so very little and inconsiderable, as to be scarce worthy of our hopes and fears, our desires and aversions, our wrath and resentments our sorrows and joys. Such a steady prospect and expectation of things infinite and everlasting, will by degrees, dissolve the force of visible and temporal things, and make them unable to raise any wild and unruly passions within us. Happy the soul that has a strong and lively faith of unseen worlds, of future terrors and glories: this will cure the vicious disorders of flesh and sense, appetite and passion: this will raise the spirit on the wings of devout affection, to the borders of paradise, and attemper the soul to the business and the joys of the blessed. *Doctrine of the Passions.*

CHILDREN SHOULD NOT BE ENCOURAGED IN CRUEL DIVERSIONS

Nor should they ever be allowed to practice those diversions that carry an idea of barbarity and cruelty in them, though it be but to brute creatures. They should not set up cocks to be banged at with cudgels thrown at them about Shrovetide; nor delight in giving a tedious lingering death to a young litter of dogs or cats, that may be appointed to be destroyed and drowned, lest they multiply too much in a house: nor should they take pleasure in pricking, cutting, or mangling young birds which they have caught, nor using any savage and bloody practices toward any creatures whatsoever; lest their hearts grow hard and unrelenting, and they learn in time to practice these cruelties upon their own kind, and to murder and torture their fellow-mortals; or at least to be indifferent to their pain and distress, so as to occasion it without remorse. *Posthumous Works.*

RELIGIOUS AND MORAL REFLECTIONS ON THE PRACTICE OF GAMING

Many young gentlemen have been there bubbled, and cheated of large sums of money, which were given them by their parents to support them honorably in their stations. In such sort of shops young ladies are tempted to squander away too large a share of their yearly allowance, if not of the provision which their parents have made for their whole lives. It is a fatal snare to both sexes: if they win, they are allured still onward, while, according to their language, luck runs on their side: if they lose, they are tempted to another and another cast of the die, and enticed on still to fresh games, by a delusive hope, that fortune will turn; and they shall recover all they have lost. In the midst of these scenes, their passions rise shamefully, a greedy desire of gain makes them warm and eager, and new losses plunge them sometimes into vexation and fury, till the soul is quite beaten off from its guard, and virtue and reason have no manner of command over them.

My worthy friend Mr. Neal, in his reformation sermon, has taken occasion not only to inform us that "merchants and tradesmen mix themselves at these tables with men of desperate fortunes, and throw the dice for their estates." But in a very decent and soft manner of address, has inquired, "Whether public gaming in virtuous ladies is not a little out of character? Whether it does not draw them into mixed company, and give them an air of boldness, which is perfectly inconsistent with that modesty which is the ornament of the fair sex? Whether it does not engage them in an habit of idleness, and of keeping ill hours? Whether their passions are not sometimes disordered? And whether the losses they sustain have not a tendency to breed ill blood in their families, and between their nearest relations? It has been often observed, that gaming in a lady has usually been attended with the loss of reputation, and sometimes of that which is still more valuable, her virtue and honor." Thus far proceeds this useful sermon.

Now, if these be the dismal and frequent consequences of the gaming-table, the loss of a little money is one of the least injuries you sustain by it. But what if you should still come off gainers? Is this the way that God has taught or allowed us to procure the necessary comforts of life? Is this a sort of labor or traffic on which you can ask the blessing of heaven? Can you lift up your face to God, and pray that he would succeed the cast of the die, the drawing of the lot, of the dealing out of the cards, so as to increase your gain, while it is the very sense and language of the prayer, that your neighbor may sustain so much loss? This is a sad and guilty circumstance which belongs to gaming, that one can gain nothing but what another loses; and consequently we cannot ask a blessing upon ourselves, but at the same time we pray for a blast upon our neighbor.

Will you hope to excuse it by saying, that my neighbor consents to this blast or this loss, by entering into the game, and there is no injury where there is consent?

I answer, that though he consents to lose conditionally and upon a venturous hope of gain, yet he is not willing to sustain the loss absolutely; but when either chance, or his neighbor's skill in the game has determined against him, then he is constrained to lose, and does it unwillingly; so that he still sustains it as a loss, or misfortune, or evil. Now, if you ask a blessing from heaven on this way of your getting money, you ask rather absolutely that your neighbor may sustain a loss, without any regard to the condition of his hope of gain. Your wish and prayer is directly that you may get, and he may lose: you cannot wish this good to yourself but you wish the contrary evil to him: and therefore I think gaming for gain cannot be consistent with the laws of Christ, which certainly forbid us to wish evil to our neighbor.

And if you cannot so much as in thought ask God's blessing upon this, as you certainly may on such recreations as have an evident tendency innocently to exercise the body and relax the mind, it seems your conscience secretly condemns it, and there is an additional proof of its being evil to you.

All the justest writers of morality, and the best casuists, have generally, if not universally, determined against those methods of gain. Whatsoever game may he indulged as lawful, it is still as a recreation, and not as a calling or business of life: and therefore no larger sums ought to be risked or ventured in this manner, than what may be lawfully laid out by any person for their present recreation, according to their different circumstances in the world.

Besides all this, think of the loss of time, and the waste of life, that is continually made by some who frequent those gaming places. Think how it calls away many a youth from their proper business, and tempts them to throw away what is not their own, and to risk the substance, as well as the displeasure of their parents, or their master, at all the uncertain hazards of a dice-box. *Posthumous Works.*

ON PUBLIC DANCING ASSEMBLIES

It is acknowledged to be proper and needful that young people should be indulged in some recreations, agreeable to their age, and suitable to the condition in which providence has placed them. But I would ask whether the great and only valuable end of recreation is to be expected from these midnight assemblies, namely to relieve us from the fatigues of life, and to exhilarate the spirits, so as thereby to fit us for the duties of life and religion? Now are these the proper means to fit us for the duties of either kind? Perhaps it will be said that dancing which is practiced in those assemblies, is an exercise conducive to health, and therefore a means of fitting us for the duties of life. But may not the unseasonableness of the midnight hour prevent and over balance the benefit, that might otherwise be supposed to arise from the exercise? Is it likely that natural health should be promoted, or preserved, by changing the seasons and order of nature, and by allotting those hours to exercise, which God and nature have ordained to rest? Is the returning home after five or six hours dancing, through the cold and damp of the midnight air, a proper means of preserving health? or rather, is it not more likely to impair and destroy it? Have not these fatal effects been too often felt? Have there not been sacrifices of human life offered to this midnight idol? Have there been no fair young martyrs to this unseasonable folly? Are there not some of its slaves who are become feeble, laboring under sore diseases, and some of them fallen asleep in death? Have not their music and their dancing, instead of natural rest in their beds, brought them down to a long silence in their grave, and an untimely rest in the bed of dust? Those amiable pieces of human nature, who were lately the joy and hope of their too indulgent parents, are now the bitterness of their hearts; and those very exercises from whence they hoped the continence of their joy, as the supposed means of confirming their children's health, are become an everlasting spring of their mourning.

And as those midnight recreations are badly suited to fit us for the duties of the civil life, so they are worse suited to fit us for, or rather, they are more apparently opposite to, the duties of religion. The religion of the closet is neglected, the beautiful regularity and order of the family is broken; and when the night has been turned into day, a good part of the next day is turned into night, while the duties of the morning, both to God and man, are unperformed. Those who have frequented these assemblies know all this, and are my witnesses to the truth of it. Nay, the very practice itself, at those unseasonable hours, tells all the world how much they prefer these dangerous amusements, to the worship of God in the evening and in the morning, and to all the conveniences and decorum of family government. Besides, if I speak to Christians, have you not found that the indulgence of this sort of diversions, which are usually practiced in those unseasonable assemblies, leads the mind away insensibly from God and religion, gives a vanity to the spirit, and greatly abates the spiritual and heavenly temper which should belong to Christians? Has it not taken away the savor of godliness and tincture of piety from some younger minds? And do elder Christians never suffer by it? Let it be further considered, what sort of company you mingle with in those midnight assemblies. Are they most frequented by the wise and pious, or by the more vain and vicious part of mankind? Do they tend to fill your mind with the most improving notions, and your ears and your lips with the most proper conversation? Do you that frequent them never find your piety in danger there? Does strict religion and prayer relish so well with you after those gaudy nights of mirth and folly? And do you then, when you join in those assemblies, practice the commands of God, to abstain from all appearance of evil, and to shun the paths of temptation? Can you pray for a blessing on your attendance on these midnight meetings? Or can you hope to run into the midst of those sparks and living coals, and yet not be burned, nor so much as have your garments singed? Are not parents very generally sensible that there are dangerous snares to youth in those gay diversions? And therefore the mother will herself go along with her young offspring to take care of them, and to watch over them; and perhaps there is scarcely any place or time which more wants the watchful eye of a superior. But here let me ask, is this all the reason why the mother attends those scenes of vanity? Has she no relish for them herself? Has she no gay humors of her own to be gratified, which she disguises and covers with the pretence of a parental solicitude for the virtue and honor of her offspring? Are there no mothers who freely lead their children into those perilous places, where soul and body are in danger, and are really, their tempters, under a color of being their guardians?

You will plead, perhaps, that some of these things are proper for the improvement of young people in good breeding and politeness. They must be brought into company, to see the world, and to learn to behave with becoming decency. Well, suppose these assemblies to be academies of politeness, and that young people attend there upon lectures of good breeding. Is there no other time so fit as midnight, to polish the youth of both sexes, and to breed them well? May not an hour or two be appointed at more proper seasons, by select companies, for mutual conversation, and innocent delight? Can there be no genteel recreations enjoyed, no lessons of behavior taught by daylight? Can no method of improvement in good breeding be contrived and appointed which shall be more secure from temptations and inconveniences? Are there none which are more harmless, more innocent, of better reputation among persons of strict piety, and which make less inroad on the duties of life, both solitary and social, civil and religious. *Posthumous Works.*

It is the duty of parents who would give their children a good education, to see to it that children, in their younger years, do not indulge such recreations as may spoil all the good effects of the pious instructions, the prayers, and cares of their parents. Otherwise, if you encourage them in such recreations, you are building up those vanities of mind, and those vicious inclinations with one hand which you labor to prevent or destroy with the other. *Posthumous Works.*

OF SECRET AND SOCIAL PRAYER

While I am discouraging young Christians from that affectation of long prayer, which arises from an ostentation of their parts, from a superstitious hope of pleasing God better by saying many words, or from a trifling frame of spirit; I would not have my readers imagine that the shortest prayers are always the best. Our sinful natures are too ready to put off God in secret or in the family, with a few minutes of worship, from mere sloth and weariness of holy things; which is equally to be blamed: for hereby we omit a great part of the necessary work of prayer in confessions, petitions, pleadings for mercy, or thanksgivings. Nor do I think that prayer in public assemblies should be short, as though the only design of it were a mere preface before the sermon, or a benediction after it. Whereas social prayer is one considerable part, if not the chief duty, of public worship; and we ought generally to continue so long in it, as to run through the most necessary and important purposes of a social address to the throne of grace. Christian prudence will teach us to determine the length of our prayers agreeably to the occasion and present circumstances, and according to the measure of our own ability for this work. *Guide to Prayer.*

OF THE TONE OF THE VOICE IN PRAYER

Though the beauty of our expressions, and the tuneableness of our voice, can never render our worship more acceptable to God, the infinite Spirit; yet our natures being composed of flesh and spirit, may be assisted in worship by the harmony of the voice of him that speaks. Should the matter, method, and expressions be never so well chosen in prayer, yet it is possible for the voice to spoil the pleasure, and injure the devotion of our fellow worshippers. When speeches of the best composure and warmest language, are recited in a cold, harsh, or ungrateful way, the beauty of them is almost lost.

Some persons, by nature, have a very sweet and tuneful voice, that whatsoever they speak appears pleasing. Others must take much more pains, and attend with diligence to rules and directions, that their voice may be formed to an agreeable pronunciation: for we find by sad experience, that all the advantages that nature can obtain or apply to assist our devotions, are all little enough to keep our hearts from wandering, and to maintain delight: at least it is a necessary duty to know and avoid those disagreeable ways of pronunciation, that may rather disgust than edify each as may join with us.

I confess, in secret prayer there is no necessity of a voice, for God hears a whisper as well as a sigh or a groan. Yet some Christians cannot pray with any advantage to themselves, without the use of a voice in some degree: nor can I judge it at all improper, but rather preferable, so that you have a convenient place for secrecy: for hereby you will not only excite your affections the more, but by practice in secret, if you take due care of your voice there, you may learn also to speak in public the better.

The great and general rule I would lay down for managing the voice in prayer is this: "Let us use the same voice with which we usually speak in grave and serious conversation, especially upon pathetical and affecting subjects." This is the best direction that I know, to regulate the sound as well as the words. Our own native and common voice appears most natural, and may be managed with the greatest ease. And some persons have taken occasion to ridicule our worship, and to censure us as hypocrites, when we fondly seek any new and different sort of sounds or voices in our prayers. *Guide to Prayer.*

THAT IT IS SINFUL TO COMPLAIN OF THE DISPENSATIONS OF PROVIDENCE

An African has no right to complain, that he was not born a Briton; nor a porter that he was not born a prince; nor Saphronius and I, that we were not made prophets and apostles. If God has furnished all men with such *natural powers*, as being improved in the best manner, would lead them to virtue, religion, and happiness, surely his creatures may give him leave to make so much distinction between them, as to set some of them in a plainer and easier road to happiness than he has others: and it is shameful ingratitude for us, in a Christian country, to complain of our bountiful Creator, who has afforded us so much peculiar favors, and made our way to heaven plainest of all. *Strength and Weakness of Human Reason.*

CHARITABLE JUDGMENT OF OUR FELLOW-CREATURES RECOMMENDED

Let us take a survey of the world, and see what a mixture there is of amiable and hateful qualities among the children of men. There is beauty and comeliness; there is vigor and vivacity; there is good humor and compassion; there is wit, and judgment, and industry, even among those that are profligate and abandoned to many vices. There is sobriety, and love, and honesty, and justice, and decency amongst men that "know not God, and believe not the gospel of our Lord Jesus." There are very few of the sons and daughters of Adam, but are possessed of something good and agreeable, either by nature or acquirement; therefore when there is a necessary occasion to mention the vices of any man, I should not speak evil of him in the gross, nor heap reproaches on him by wholesale. It is very disingenuous to talk scandal in superlatives, as though every man who was a sinner, was a perfect villain, the very worst of men, all over hateful and abominable.

How sharply should our own thoughts reprove us, when we give our pride and malice a loose to ravage over all the characters of our neighbors, and deny all that is good concerning them, because they have something in them that is criminal and worthy of blame! Thus our judgment is abused by our passions; and sometimes this folly reigns in us to such a degree, that we can hardly allow a man to be wise or ingenuous, to have a grain of good sense, or good humor, that is not of our profession, or our party, in matters or church or state. Let us look back upon our conduct, and blush to think that we should indulge such prejudices, such sinful partiality. *Sermons, vol.* 1.

I will not therefore say within myself concerning any man, "I hate him utterly, and abhor him in all respects, because he has not true holiness." But I will look upon him, and consider whether there may not be some accomplishment in him, some moral virtue, some valuable talent, some natural or acquired excellency; and I will not neglect to pay due esteem to every deserving quality, wheresoever I find it. It is a piece of honor due to God our Creator, to observe the various signatures of his wisdom that he has impressed upon his creatures, and the overflowing treasures of his goodness, which he has distributed among the works of his hands.

Thus I may very justly love a man, for whom, in the vulgar sense, I have no charity, that is, such a one as I believe to be in a state of sin and death, and have no present hope of his salvation. How could holy parents fulfill their duties of affection to their wicked children? Or pious children pay due respect to sinful parents? How could a believer fulfill the law of love to an unbelieving brother, or dearer relative, if we ought to admit of no love to persons that are in a state of enmity to God? *Sermons, vol.* 1.

ANCIENT AND MODERN EDUCATION CONTRASTED

So weak and unhappy is human nature, that it is ever ready to run into extremes; and when we would recover ourselves from an excess on the right hand, we know not where to stop, till we are got to an excess on the left. Instances of this kind are innumerable in all the affairs of human life; but it is hardly more remarkable in any thing, than in the strict and severe education of our fathers a century ago, and in the most profuse and unlimited liberty that is indulged to children in our age.

In those days the sons were bred up to learning by terrible discipline: every Greek and Latin author they conversed with, was attended by one or many new scourges, to drive them into acquaintance with him; and not the least misdemeanor in life could escape the lash; as though the father would prove his daily *love to his son,* by never *sparing his rod.*[1] Nowadays young master must be treated with a foolish fondness, till he has grown to the size of man: and let his faults be never so heinous, and his obstinacy never so great, yet the preceptor must not let him hear the name of the rod, lest the child should be frighted or hurt; the advice of the wisest of men is utterly forgotten, when he tells us, that due *correction shall drive out the folly that is bound up in the heart of a child.*[2] Or else they boldly reverse his divine counsel,[3] as though they would make the rule of their practice a direct contradiction to the words of Solomon, namely, that *he that* spareth *the rod loveth his son, but he that* hateth *him, chastens him betimes.*

In that day many children were kept in a most servile subjection, and not suffered to sit down, or to speak, in the presence of their father, till they were come to the age of one and twenty. The least degree of freedom was esteemed a bold presumption, and incurred a sharp reproof. Now they are made familiar companions to their parents, almost from the very nursery; and therefore they will hardly bear a cheek or rebuke at their hand.

In the beginning of the last century, and so onward to the middle of it, the children were usually obliged to believe what their parents and their masters taught them, whether they were principles of science, or articles of faith and practice; they were tied down almost to every punctilio, as though it was necessary to salvation; they were not suffered to examine or inquire whether their teachers were in the right, and scarce knew upon what grounds they were to assent to the things that were taught them; for it was a maxim of all teachers, that the learner must believe: *Discentem operte credere.* Then an *ipse dixit,* or Aristotle said so, was a sufficient proof of any proposition in the colleges; and for a man of five and twenty to be a Christian and a Protestant, a dissenter or a churchman, it was almost reason

1 Proverbs 13:24.
2 Proverbs 22:15.
3 Proverbs 13:24.

enough to say that his father was so. But in this century, when the
doctrine of a just and reasonable liberty is better known, too many
of the present youth break all the bonds of nature and duty, and
run to the wildest degrees of looseness, both in belief and practice.
They slight the religion which their parents have taught them, that
they may appear to have chosen a religion for themselves: and when
they have made a creed or belief of their own, or rather borrowed
some scraps of infidelity from their vain companions and equals,
they find pretences enough to cast off all other creeds at once, as
well as the counsels and customs of their religious predecessors.

"The practices of our fathers," say they, "were precise and foolish, and shall be no rule for our conduct; the articles of their faith
were absurd and mysterious, but we will believe nothing of mystery,
lest our faith should be as ridiculous as theirs." In their younger
years, and before their reason is half grown, they pretend to examine the sublimest doctrines of Christianity; and a raw and half-wit-
ted boy shall commence an infidel, because he cannot comprehend
some of the glorious truths of the gospel, and laughs at his elders
and his ancestors, for believing what they could not comprehend.

The child nowadays forgets that his parents are obliged by all
the laws of God and nature, to train him up in his own religion, till
he has come to the proper age of discretion to judge for himself; he
forgets, or he will not know, that the parent is entrusted with the
care of the souls of his young offspring by the very laws of nature,
as well as by the revealed covenants of innocency and of grace. The
son nowadays forgets the obligations he is under to honor and obey
the persons that gave him birth; he pays no regard to the doctrines
which led on his ancestors to the love of God and man; whereas
doctrines that have such influence, claim at least some degrees of
attention, and especially from a son who has been trained up in
them, and beheld the effect of them in the piety of his parents; nor
will the very light of nature suffer him to depart from them, but
upon the clearest judgment of his own mature reason, a thorough
and impartial search into the subject, the loud inward dictates of his

conscience, and the full evidence of his parents' mistake.

So wanton and licentious a spirit has possessed some of the youth of the nation, that they never think they have freed themselves from the prejudices of their education, till they have thrown off almost all the yokes of restraint that are laid upon them by God or man. Some take a petulant pride in laying aside the Holy Scriptures, for the same reason that Timothy was advised to *continue in them*, and that is, because *they have learned and known them from their very childhood.*[1] And some, perhaps, have been laughed out of their Christianity, lest it should be said, their mothers and their nurses made them Christians.

Heretofore the sons were scarce suffered to be absent from home an hour, without express leave, till they were arrived to the age of man, nor daughters till they were married; now both sexes take an unbounded license of roving where they please, and from a dozen years old, they forget to ask leave to wander or to visit where their fancies lead them: at first the parent gives a loose and winks at it, and then the child claims it as his due for ever.

In short, the last age taught mankind to believe that they were mere children, and treated them as such, till they were near thirty years old; but the present gives them leave to fancy themselves complete men and women at twelve or fifteen; and they accordingly judge and manage for themselves entirely, and too often despise all advice of their elders.

Now though it be sufficiently evident that both these are extremes of liberty, or restraint, yet if we judge by the reason of things, or by experience and success, surely the ancient education is to be preferred before the present, and of the two should rather be chosen. *Posthumous Works.*

EXTREMES OF LIBERTY AND RESTRAINT TO BE AVOIDED IN THE EDUCATION OF YOUTH

But after all, is there no medium between these two extremes,

---

1 2 Timothy 3:15.

excess of confinement and excess of liberty? May not young under-standings be allowed to shoot and spread themselves a little, with-out growing rank and rampant? May not children be kept in due and gentle subjection to their parents, without putting yokes of bondage upon them? Is there no reasonable restraint of the wild opinions, and violent inclinations of youth, without making chains for the understanding, and throwing fetters on the soul? May not the young gentleman begin to act like a man, without forgetting that he is a son? And maintain the full liberty of his own judgment, without insolence and contempt of the opinions of his elders? May not he who is bred up a Protestant and a Christian judge freely for himself, without the prejudices of his education, and yet continue a Christian and a Protestant still? Is it not possible for the parent to indulge, and the child to enjoy a just liberty, and yet neither encour-age nor practice a wild licentiousness?

Yes, surely; and there have been happy instances in the last age, and there are some in this, both of parents and children, that have learned to tread this middle path, and found wisdom and virtue in it, piety and peace. Agathus has bred his son up under such discipline, as renders them both proper examples to the world. *Posthumous Works.*

THE END OF TIME

And the angel which I saw stand upon the sea, and upon the earth, lifted up his hand to heaven, and sware by him that liveth for ever and ever, that there shall be time no longer.[1] This is the oath and solemn sentence of a mighty angel who came down from heaven, and by the description of him in the first verse, he seems to be the *Angel of God's presence, in whom is the name of God*, even our Lord Jesus Christ himself, who pronounced and sware that *time shall be no longer;* for all seasons and times are now put into his hand, together with the book of his Father's decrees.[2] What special

---

1 Revelation 10:5, 6.
2 Revelation 5:7, 9.

age or period of time in this world the prophecy refers to, may not be so easy to determine; but this is certain, that it may be happily applied to the period of every man's life; for whensoever the term of our continuance in this world is finished, *our time* in the present circumstances and scenes that attend it *shall be no more;* we shall be swept off the stage of this visible state into an unseen and eternal world: eternity comes upon us at once, and all that we enjoy, all that we do, and all that we suffer in *time, shall be no more. World to Come.*

The moment is hastening upon us, when the mighty angel who manages the affairs of the kingdom of providence, shall swear concerning every unbelieving and impenitent sinner, that the *time of offered mercy shall be no longer, the time of pardon and grace and reconciliation shall be no more:* the sound of this mercy reaches not the regions of the dead; those who die before they are reconciled, they die under the load of their sins, and must perish for ever, without the least hope or glimpse of reconciling or forgiving grace. *World to Come.*

THE INESTIMABLE VALUE OF TIME

Every hour you live, is an hour given you to prepare for dying, and to save a soul. If you were but apprized of the worth of your own souls, you would better know the worth of days and hours, and of every passing moment, for they are given to secure your immortal interest, and save a soul from everlasting misery. And you would be zealous and importunate in the prayer of Moses, the man of God, upon the meditation of the shortness of life. "So teach us to number our days as to apply our hearts to wisdom,"[1] *i.e.* So teach us to consider how few and uncertain our days are, that we may be truly wise in preparing for the end of them.

It is a matter of vast importance to be ever ready for the end of time, ready to hear this awful sentence confirmed with the oath of the glorious angel, that *time shall be no longer.* The terrors or the comforts of a dying bed depend upon it; the solemn and decisive

---

1 Psalm 90:12.

voice of judgment depends upon it; the joys and the sorrows of a long eternity depend upon it. Go now, careless sinner, and in the view of such things as these, go and trifle away time as you have done before: time, that invaluable treasure: go and venture the loss of your souls, and the hopes of heaven and your eternal happiness, in wasting away the remnant of hours or moments of life: but remember the awful voice of the angel is hastening towards you, and the sound is just breaking upon you, that *time shall be no longer. World to Come.*

THE CHURCH-YARD

What a number of hillocks of death appear all round us! What are the tombstones, but memorials of the inhabitants of that town, to inform us of the period of all their lives, and to point out the day when it was said to each of them, *Your time shall be no longer.* O, may I readily learn this important lesson, that my turn is hastening too; such a little hillock shall shortly arise for me in some unknown spot of ground; it shall cover this flesh and these bones of mine in darkness, and shall hide them from the light of the sun, and from the sight of man, till the heavens shall be no more.

Perhaps some kind surviving friend may engrave my name with the number of my days, upon a plain funeral stone, without ornament, and below envy; there shall my tomb stand among the rest, as a fresh monument of the frailty of nature and the end of time. It is possible some friendly foot may now and then visit the place of my repose, and some tender eye may bedew the cold memorial with a tear: one or another of my old acquaintance may possibly attend there to learn the silent lecture of mortality from my gravestone, which my lips are now preaching aloud to the world: and if love and sorrows should reach so far, perhaps while his soul is melting in his eye-lids, and his voice scarce finds an utterance, he will point with his finger, and show his companion the month and the day of my decease. O, that solemn, that awful day, which shall finish my appointed time on earth, and put a final period to all the designs of my heart, and all the labors of my tongue and pen!

Think, O my soul, that while friends or strangers are engaged on the spot, and reading the date of my departure hence, thou wilt be fixed under a decisive and unchangeable sentence, rejoicing in the rewards of time well improved, or suffering the longer sorrows which shall attend the abuse of it, in an unknown world of happiness or misery. *World to Come.*

GUILT AND INNOCENCE

Danger of guilt stands near the extreme limits of innocence. *World to Come.*

THE DANGER OF LATE REPENTANCE

It is a wise and just observation among Christians, though it is a very common one, that the Scriptures give us *one* instance of a penitent saved in his dying hour, and that is the thief upon the cross, that so none might utterly despair: but there is *but one* such instance given, that none might presume. The work of repentance is too difficult, and too important a thing, to be left to the languors of a dying bed, and the tumults and flutterings of thought, which attend such a late conviction. There can be hardly any effectual proofs given of the sincerity of such repentings: and I am verily persuaded there are few of them sincere; for we have often found those violent emotions of the conscience vanish again, if the sinner has happened to recover his health; they seem to be merely the wild perplexities and struggles of nature, averse to misery rather than averse to sin: their renouncing their former lusts, on the very borders of hell and destruction, is more like the vehement efforts of a drowning creature, constrained to let go a most beloved object, and taking eager hold of any plank for safety, rather than the calm, and reasonable, and voluntary designs of a mariner, who forsakes his early joys, ventures himself in a ship that is offered him, and sets sail for the heavenly country. I never will pronounce such efforts and endeavors desperate, lest I limit the grace of God, which is unbounded; but I can give very little encouragement for hope to an hour or two of this vehement and tumultuous penitence, on the very brink of damnation. *Judas repented*, but his agonies of soul hurried him to hasten his own death, *that he might go to his own place:* and there is abundance of such kind of repenting in every corner of hell; that is a deep and dreadful pit, whence there is no redemption, though there are millions of such sort of penitents; it is a strong and dark prison, where no beam of comfort ever shines, where bitter anguish and mourning for sins past, is no evangelical repentance, but everlasting and hopeless sorrow. *World to Come.*

VANITY INSCRIBED ON ALL THINGS

Time, like a long flowing stream, makes haste into eternity, and is for ever lost and swallowed up there; and while it is hastening to its period, it sweeps away all things with it which are not immortal. There is a limit appointed by providence, to the duration of all the pleasant and desirable scenes of life, to all the works of the hands of men, with all the glories and excellences of animal nature, and all that is made of flesh and blood. Let us not doat upon any thing here below, for heaven has inscribed vanity upon it. The moment is hastening when the decree of heaven shall be uttered, and providence shall pronounce upon every glory of the earth, "Its time shall be no longer."

What is that stately building, that princely palace, which now entertains and amuses our sight with ranks of marble columns, and wide-spreading arches; that gay edifice, which enriches our imagination with a thousand royal ornaments, and a profusion of costly and glittering furniture? Time and all its circling hours, with a swift wing are brushing it away; decay steals upon it insensibly, and a few years hence it shall lie in moldering ruin and desolation. Unhappy possessor, if he has no better inheritance!

What are those fine and elegant gardens, those delightful walks, those gentle ascents, and soft declining slopes, which raise and sink the eye by turns to a thousand vegetable pleasures? How lovely are those sweet borders, and those growing varieties of bloom and fruit, which recall lost paradise to mind? Those living parterres which regale the sense with vital fragrancy, and make glad the sight by their refreshing verdure and intermingled flowery beauties? The scythe of time is passing over them all: they wither, they die away, they drop and vanish into dust: their duration is short; a few months deface all their yearly glories, and within a few years, perhaps all these rising terrace-walks, these gentle verging declivities, shall lose all order and elegance, and become a rugged heap of ruins: those well distinguish borders and parterres shall be levelled in confusion, and thrown into common earth again, for the ox and the ass to graze upon them. Unhappy man, who possesses this agreeable spot of ground, if he has no paradise more durable than this!

And no wonder that these labors of the hands of men should perish, when even the works of God are perishable.

What are these visible heavens, these lower skies, and this globe of earth? They are indeed the glorious workmanship of the Almighty. But they are waxing old, and waiting their period too, when the angel shall pronounce upon them, that *time shall be no more*. The heavens "shall be folded up as a vesture, the elements of the lower world shall melt with fervent heat, and the earth and all the works thereof, shall be burnt up with fire." May the unruinable world be but my portion, and the heaven of heavens my inheritance, which is built for an eternal mansion for the sons of God: these buildings shall out live time and nature, and exist through unknown ages of felicity!

What have we mortals to be proud of in our present state, when every human glory is so fugitive and fading? Let the brightest and the best of us say to ourselves, that we are but dust and vanity.

Is my body formed upon a graceful model? Are my limbs well turned, and my complexion better colored than my neighbor's? Beauty even in perfection is of shortest date; a few years will inform me that its bloom vanishes, its flower withers, its luster grows dim, its duration shall be no longer; and if life be prolonged, yet the pride and glory of it is for ever lost in age and wrinkles: or perhaps our vanity meets a speedier fate. Death and the grave, with a sovereign and irresistible command, summon the brightest as well as the coarsest pieces of human nature, to lie down early in their cold embraces; and at last they must all mix together among worms and corruption. Aesop the deformed, and Helena the fair, are lost and undistinguished from common earth. Nature in its gayest bloom, is but a painted vanity.

Are my nerves well strung and vigorous? Is my activity and strength far superior to my neighbor's in the days of youth? But youth has its appointed limit: age steals upon it, unstrings the nerves, and makes the force of nature languish into infirmity and feebleness. Sampson and Goliah would have lost their boasted advantages of stature, and their brawny limbs, in the course of half a century, though the one had escaped the sling of David, and the other the vengeance of his own hands in the ruin of Dagon's temple. Man, in his best estate, is a flying shadow and vanity.

Even those nobler powers of human life, which seem to have something angelic in them, I mean the powers of wit and fancy, gay imagination and capacious memory, they are all subject to the same laws of decay and death. What though they can raise and animate beautiful scenes in a moment, and in imitation of creating power, can spread bright appearances and new worlds before the senses and souls of their friends? What though they can entertain the better part of mankind, the refined and polite world, with high delight and rapture? These scenes of rapturous delight grow flat and old by a frequent review, and the very powers that raised them grow feeble apace. What though they can give immortal applause and fame to their possessors? It is but the immortality of an empty name, a mere succession of the breath of men; and it is a short sort of immortality too, which must die and perish when this world parishes. A poor shadow of duration indeed, while the real period of these powers is hastening every day; they languish and die as fast as animal nature, which has a large share in them, makes haste to its decay; and the time of their exercise shall shortly be no more.

In vain the aged poet or the painter would call up the muse and genius of their youth, and summon all the arts of their imagination, to spread and dress out some visionary scene. In vain the elegant orator would recall the bold and masterly figures, and all those flowery images which gave ardor, grace, and dignity to his younger composures, and charmed every ear: they are gone, they are fled beyond the reach of their owner's call: their time is past, they are vanished and lost beyond all hope of recovery.

The God of nature has pronounced an unpassable period upon all the powers, and pleasures, and glories of this mortal state. Let us then be afraid to make any of them our boast or our happiness; but point our affections to those diviner objects whose nature is everlasting; let us seek those religious attainments, and those new-created powers of a sanctified mind, concerning which it shall never be pronounced that their *time shall be no longer.*

O may every one of us humbly be content, at the call of heaven, to part with all that is pleasing or magnificent here on earth; let us resign even these agreeable talents when the God of nature demands; and when the hour arrives, that shall close our eyes to all visible things, and lay our fleshly structure in the dust; let us yield up our whole selves to the hands of our creator, who shall reserve our spirits with himself; and while we cheerfully give up all that was mortal to the grave, we may lie down full of the joyful hope of a rising immortality. New and unknown powers and glories, brighter flames of imagination, richer scenes of wit and fancy, and diviner talents, are preparing for us when we shall awake from the dust; and the mind itself shall have all its faculties in a sublime state of improvement. These shall make us equal, if not superior, to angels, for we are nearer akin to the Son of God than they are, and therefore we shall be made more like him. *Posthumous Works.*

OF PRAYER

Prayer is a secret and appointed means to obtain all the blessings that we want, whether they relate to this life, or the life to come; and shall we not know, how to use the means God has appointed for our happiness? Shall so glorious a privilege lie unimproved through our own neglect?

Were the business of prayer nothing else but to come and beg mercy of God, it would be the duty of every man to know how to draw up such petitions: but prayer is a work of much larger extent. When a holy soul comes before God, he has much more to say than merely to beg. He tells his God what a sense he has of the divine attributes, and what high esteem he pays to his Majesty, his wisdom, his power, and his mercy. He talks with him about the works of creation, and stands wrapped up in wonder. He talks about the grace and mystery of redemption, and is yet more filled with admiration and joy. He talks of all the affairs, of nature, grace, and glory; he speaks of his works of providence, of love, and vengeance, in this and the future world. Infinite and glorious are the subjects of this holy communion between God and his saints: and shall we content ourselves with sighs and groans, and a few short wishes, and deprive our souls of so rich, so divine, so glorious a pleasure, for want of knowing how to furnish out such meditations, and to speak this blessed language.

How excellent and valuable is this skill of prayer, in comparison of the many meaner arts and accomplishments of human nature that we labor night and day to obtain? What toil do men daily undergo for seven years together, to acquire the knowledge of a trade and business in this present life. Now the greatest part of the business between us and heaven is transacted in the way of prayer: with how much more diligence should we seek the knowledge of this heavenly commerce, than any thing that concerns us merely on earth? How many years of our short life are spent to learn the Greek, the Latin, and the French tongues, that we may hold correspondence abroad among the living nations, and converse with the writings of the dead? And shall not the language wherein we converse with heaven and the living God, be thought worth equal pains? How nicely do some persons study the art of conversation, that they may be accepted in all companies, and share in the favor of men? Is not the same care due, to seek all methods of acceptance with God, that we may approve ourselves in his presence? What a high value is set upon human oratory, or the art of persuasion, whereby we are fitted to discourse and prevail with our fellow creatures? And is this art of divine oratory of no esteem with us, which teaches us to utter our inward breathings of the soul, and plead and prevail with our Creator, through the assistance of the Holy Spirit, and the mediation of our Lord Jesus?

O, let the excellency and high value of this gift of prayer engage our earnestness and endeavors in proportion to its superior dignity: let us "covet the best of gifts" with the warmest desire, and pray for them with, ardent supplication.[1]

Another argument may be borrowed from our very character and profession as Christians; some measure of the gift of prayer is of great necessity and universal use to all that are called by the name.

Shall we profess to be followers of Christ, and not know how to speak to the Father? Are we commanded to pray always, and upon all occasions, to be constant and fervent in it, and shall we be contented with ignorance and incapacity to obey this command? Are we invited by the warmest exhortations, and encouraged by the highest hopes to draw near to God with all our wants and sorrows, and shall we not learn to express those wants, and pour out those sorrows before the Lord? Is there a way made for our access to the throne by the blood and intercession of Jesus Christ, and shall we not know how to form a prayer to be sent to heaven, and spread before the throne by his glorious intercession? Is his Holy Spirit promised to teach us to pray, and shall a Christian be careless or unwilling to receive such divine teachings?

There is not any faculty in the whole Christian life that is called out into so frequent exercise as this; and it is a most unhappy thing to be always at a loss to perform the work which daily necessity requires, and daily duty demands. Will a person profess to be a

1 1 Corinthians 12:18.

scholar, that cannot read? Shall any man pretend to be a minister, that cannot preach? And it is but a poor pretence we make to Christianity, if we are not able, at least in secret, to supply ourselves with a few meditations or expressions, to continue a little in this work of prayer. *Guide to Prayer.*

DEGENERACY OF HUMAN NATURE

Let us further suppose, what is sufficiently evident to our daily observation and experience, that all mankind are now a degenerate, feeble, and unhappy race of beings, that we are become sinners in the sight of God, and exposed to his anger: it is manifest enough, that this whole world is a fallen, sinful and rebellious province of God's dominion, and under the actual displeasure of its righteous Creator and Governor. The over-spreading deluge of folly and error, iniquity and misery, that covers the face of the earth, gives abundant ground for such a supposition. The experience of every man on earth affords a strong and melancholy proof, that our reasoning powers are easily led away into mistake and falsehood, wretchedly bribed and biassed by prejudices, and daily overpowered by some corrupt appetites or passions, and our wills led astray to choose evil instead of good. The best of us sometimes break the laws of our Maker, by contradicting the rules of piety and virtue which our own reason and consciences suggest to us "There is none righteous" perfectly; "no not one." Nor is there one person upon earth free from troubles and difficulties, and pains and sorrows, such as testify some resentment of our Maker.

Even from our infancy, our diseases, pains and sorrows begin, and it is very remarkably evident in some families, that these pains and diseases are propagated to the offspring, as they were contracted by the vices of the parents: and particular vicious inclinations, as well as particular distempers, are conveyed from parents to children sometimes through several generations. The best of us are not free from irregular propensities and passions even in the younger parts of life, and as our years advance, our sins break out, and continue more or less through all our lives. Our whole race then is plainly degenerate, sinful and guilty before God, and are under some tokens of his anger. *Strength and Weakness of Human Reason.*

VARIOUS DEGREES OF GUILT AND PUNISHMENT

As there is infinite variety of degrees of guilt in particular persons, and their conduct in this world, there shall be the same variety of the degrees of punishment in the world to come. Every man shall be judged according to the advantages he enjoyed. More is required from those whose advantages were greater, and their guilt is more heinous in abusing or neglecting them. God, the all-knowing and the righteous, will weigh every circumstance, both of his favors and of our use or abuse of them, in the nicest balance, and his sentence shall bear an exact proportion to the demerits of every sinner. "He that knew not his master's will, shall be beaten but with few stripes," in comparison with those criminals who knew it, and fought against it. Suppose therefore that the punishment of these rudest and most stupid nations upon the earth, in the future world, shall be exceedingly small, in proportion to the very small degrees of light and knowledge which they have enjoyed, or which have lain fairly and practically within their reach; will not this greatly relieve the difficulty?

And if even these lightest punishments which shall be assigned to the most ignorant part of the Heathen world, should be thought something severe, yet none can be thought utterly unjust, if, as was before observed, none are punished, but for acting in some measure against the light of their own minds. *Strength and Weakness of Human Reason.*

THE RAKE REFORMED IN THE HOUSE OF MOURNING

Florino was young and idle; he gave himself up to all the diversions of the town, and roved wild among all the pleasures of sense; nor did he confine himself within the limits of virtue, or withhold his heart from any forbidden joy. Often has he been heard to ridicule marriage, and affirm that no man can mourn heartily for a dead wife, for then he has leave by the law to choose a new companion, to riot in all the gayer scenes of a new courtship, and perhaps to advance his fortune too.

When he heard of the death of Serena, "Well" said he, "I will go visit my friend Lucius, and rally him a little on this occasion." He went the next day in all the wantonness of his heart to fulfill his design, inhuman and barbarous as it was, and to sport with solemn sorrow. But when Lucius appeared, the man of gaiety was strangely surprised; he saw such a sincere and inimitable distress sitting on his countenance, and discovering itself in every air and action, that he dropped his cruel purpose, his soul began to melt, and he assumed the comforter.

Fiorino's methods of consolation were all drawn from two topics: some from fate and necessity, advising an heroic indolence about unavoidable events, which are past and cannot be reversed; and some were derived from the various amusements of life, which call the soul abroad, and divide and scatter the thoughts, and suffer not the mind to attend to its inward anguish. "Come, Lucius," said he, "come, smooth your brows a little, and brighten up for an hour or two: come along with me to a concert this evening, where you shall hear some of the best pieces of music that were ever composed, and performed by some of the best hands that ever touched an instrument. Tomorrow I will wait on you to the play, or, if you please, to the new opera, where the scenes are so surprising and so gay, they would almost tempt an old hermit from his beloved cell, and call back his years to three and twenty. Come, my friend, what have the living to do with the dead? Do but forget your grievances a little, and they will die too; come, shake off the spleen, divert your heart with the entertainments of wit and melody, and call away your fancy from these gloomy and useless contemplations." Thus he ran on in his own way of talking, and opened to his mourning friend the best springs of comfort that he was acquainted with.

Lucius endured this prattle as long as he was able to endure it, but it had no manner of influence to staunch the bleeding wound, or to abate his smarting sorrows. His pain waxed more intense by such sort of applications, and the grief grew too unruly to contain itself.

Lucius then asked leave to retire a little: Florino followed him softly at a distance to the door of his closet, where indeed he observed not any of the rules of civility or just decency, but placed himself near enough to hear how the passion took its vent: and there he heard the distressed Lucius mourning over Serena's death in such language as this:

"What did Florino talk about? Necessity and fate? Alas, this is my misery, that so painful an event cannot be reversed, that the divine will has made it fate: and there is a necessity of my enduring it.

"Plays, and music, and operas! what poor trifles are these to give ease to a wounded heart! to a heart that has lost its choicest half! a heart that lies bleeding in deep anguish under such a keen parting stroke, and the long, long absence of my Serena! She is gone. The desire of my eyes and the delight of my soul is gone. The first of earthly comforts and the best of mortal blessings. She is gone, and she has taken with her all that was pleasant, all that could brighten the gloomy hours of life, that could soften the cares and relieve the burdens of it. She is gone, and the best portion and joy of my life is departed. Will she never return, never come back and bless my eyes again? No; never, never.—She will no more come back to visit this wretched world, and to dry these weeping eyes. That best portion of my life that dearest blessing is gone, and will return no more. Sorrows in long succession await me while I live; all my future days are marked out for grief and darkness.

"Let the man who feels no inward pain at the loss of such a partner, dress his dwelling in black shades and dismal formalities: Let him draw the curtains of darkness around him, and teach his chambers a fashionable mourning: but real anguish of heart needs none of these modish and dissembled sorrows. My soul is hung round with dark images in all her apartments, and every scene is sincere lamentation and death.

"I thought once I had some pretence to the courage of a man: but this is a season of untried distress: I now shudder at a thought, I start at shadows, my spirits are sunk, and horror has taken hold of me.

I feel passions in me that were unknown before; love has its own proper grief and its peculiar anguish. Mourning love has those agonies and those sinkings of spirit which are known only to bereaved and virtuous lovers.

"I stalk about like a ghost in musing silence, till the gathering sorrow grows too big for the heart, and bursts out into weak and unmanly wailings. Strange and overwhelming stroke indeed! It has melted all the man within me down to softness: my nature is gone back to childhood again: I would maintain the dignity of my age and my sex, but these eyes rebel and betray me; the eyelids are full, they overflow; the drops of love and grief trickle down my cheeks, and plow the furrows of age there before their time.

"How often in a day are these sluices opened afresh? The sight of every friend that knew her, call up my weakness and betrays my frailty. I am quite ashamed of myself. What shall I do? Is there nothing of manhood left about my heart? I will resist the passions, I will struggle with nature, I will grow indolent and forbid my tears. Alas poor feeble wretch that I am! In vain I struggle; in vain I resist: the assumed indolence vanishes; the real passion works within, it swells and bears down all before it: the torrent rises and prevails hourly, and nature will have its way. Even the Son of God, when he became man, was found weeping at the tomb of a darling friend. Lazarus died and Jesus wept.

"O my soul, what shall I do to relieve this heartache? How shall I cure this painful sensibility? Is there no opiate will reach it? Whither shall I go to leave my sorrows behind me? I wander from one room to another, and wherever I go I still seem to seek her, but I miss her still. My imagination flatters me with her lovely image, and tempts me to doubt, is she dead indeed? My fond imagination would fain forget her death bed, and impose upon my hope that I shall find her somewhere. I visit her apartment, I steal into her closet: in days past when I have missed her in her parlor, how often have I found the dear creature in that beloved corner of the house, that sweet place of divine retirement and converse with heaven?

But even that closet is empty now. I go thither, and I retire in disappointment and confusion.

"I think I should meet her in some of her walks, in some of her family cares, or her innocent amusements: I should see her face, I think, I should hear her voice and exchange a tender word or two. Ah foolish rovings of a distressed and disquieted fancy! Every room is empty and silent; closet, parlor, chambers, all empty, all silent; and that very silence and emptiness proclaim my sorrows: even emptiness and deep silence join to confess the painful loss.

"Shall I try then to put her quite out of my thoughts, since she will come no more within the reach of my senses? Shall I loosen the fair picture and drop it from my heart, since the fairer original is for ever gone? Go, then, fair picture, go from my bosom, and appear to my soul no more. Hard word! but it must be done: go, depart, thou dearest form; thou most lovely of images, go from my heart; thy presence is now too painful in that tender part of me. O unhappy word! Thy presence painful? A dismal change indeed! When thou were wont to arise and show thyself there, graces and joys were wont to arise and show themselves: graces and joys went always with her: nor did her image ever appear without them, till that dark and bitter day that spread the veil of death over her: but her image dressed in that gloomy veil, has lost all the attendant joys and graces. Let her picture vanish from my soul, then, since it has lost those endearing attendants: let it vanish away into forgetfulness, for death has robbed it of every grace and every joy.

"Yet stay a little there, tempting image, let me once more survey thee: stay a little moment, and let me take one last glance, one solemn farewell. Is there not something in the resemblance of her too lovely still to have it quite banished from my heart? Can I set my soul at work to try to forget her? Can I deal so unkindly with one who would never have forgotten me? Can my soul live without her image on it? Is it not stamped there too deep ever to be effaced?

"I think I feel all my heart-strings wrapped around her, and grow so fast to that dear picture in my fancy, they seem to be rooted there.

To be divided from it is to die. Why should I then pursue so vain and fruitless an attempt? What? forget myself? forget my life? No; it cannot be; nor can I bear to think of such a rude and cruel treatment of an image so much deserving and so much beloved. Neither passion nor reason permits me to forget her, nor is it within my power. She is present almost to all my thoughts; she is with me in all my motions; grief has arrows with her name upon them, that stick as fast and as deep as those of love; they cleave to my vitals wheresoever I go, but with a quicker sensation and a keener pain. Alas, it is love and grief together, that have shot all their arrows into my heart, and filled every vein with acute anguish and long distress.

"Where then shall I fly to find solace and ease? I cannot depart from myself: I cannot abandon these tender and smarting sensations. Shall I quit the house and all the apartments of it which renew her dear memory? Shall I rove in these open fields which lie near my dwelling, and spread wide their pleasing verdure? Shall I give my soul a loose to all nature that smiles around me, or shall I confine my daily walk to this shady and delightful garden? Oh, no; neither of these will relieve my anguish. Serena has too often blessed me with her company both in this garden and in these fields. Her very name seems written on every tree: I shall think of her and fancy I see her in every step I take. Here she pressed the grass with her feet, here she gathered violets and roses and refreshing herbs, and gave the lovely collection of sweetness into my hand. But, alas, the sweetest violet and the fairest rose is fallen, is withered, and is no more. Farewell then, ye fields and gardens, with all your varieties of green and flowery joys! Ye are all a desert, a barren wilderness, since Serena has for ever left you and will be seen there no more.

"But can friends do nothing to comfort a mourner? Come, my wise friends, surround me and divert my cares with your agreeable conversation. Can books afford no relief? Come, my books, ye volumes of knowledge, ye labors of the learned dead; come, fill up my hours with some soothing amusement. I call my better friends about me, I fly to the heroes and the philosophers of ancient ages to employ my soul among them. But, alas! neither learning nor books amuse me, nor green and smiling prospects of nature delight me, nor conversation with my wisest and best friends can entertain me in these dark and melancholy hours. Solitude, solitude in some unseen corner, some lonely grotto overgrown with shades, this is my dearest choice; let me dwell in my beloved solitude where none shall come near me; midnight and solitude are the most pleasing things to a man who is weary of daylight and of all the scenes of this visible and busy world. I would eat and drink and dwell alone, though this lonesome humor soothes and gratifies the painful passion, and gives me up to the tyranny of my sharpest sorrows. Strange mixture that I am made of! I mourn and grieve even to death, and yet I seem fond of nothing but grief and mourning.

"Woe is me! Is there nothing on earth can divert, nothing relieve me? Then let my thoughts ascend to paradise and heaven, there shall I find her better part, and grief must not enter there. From this hour take a new turn, O my soul, and never think of Serena but as shining and rejoicing among the spirits of the blest, and in the presence of her God. Rise often in holy meditation to the celestial world, and betake thyself to more intense piety. Devotion has wings that will bear thee high above the tumults and passions of lower life; devotion will direct and speed thy flight to a country of brighter scenes.

"Shake off this earthliness of mind, this dust of mortality that hangs about thee; rise upward often in an hour, and dwell much in those regions where thy devout partner is gone; thy better half is safely arrived there, and that world knows nothing but joy and love.

"She is gone; the prophets and the apostles and the best of departed souls have marked out her way to heaven: bear witness, ye apostles and holy prophets, ye best of departed souls bear witness that I am seeking to follow her in the appointed moment. Let the wheels of nature and time roll on apace in their destined way. Let suns and moons arise and set apace, and light a lonesome travel-ler onward to his home. Blessed Jesus! be thou my living leader!

Virtue, and the track of my Serena's feet, be my daily and delightful path. The track leads upward to the regions of love and joy. How can I dare to wander from the path of virtue, lest I lose that beloved track? Remember, O my soul, her footsteps are found in no other road.

"If my love to virtue should ever fail me, the steps of my Serena would mark out my way, and help to secure me from wandering. O may the kind influences of heaven descend from above and establish and guard my pious resolutions! May the divine powers of religion be my continual strength, and the hope of eternal things my never failing support, till I am dismissed from this prison of the flesh and called to ascend to the spirits of the just made perfect, till I bid adieu to all that is not immortal, and go dwell with my God and my adored Saviour; there shall I find my lost Serera again, and share with her the unutterable joys of paradise."

Here Lucius thew himself on the couch, and lay silent in profound meditation.

When Florino had heard all this mournful rhapsody, he retired and stole away in secret, for he was now utterly ashamed of his first barbarous design: he felt a sort of strange sympathy of sorrow, such as he never knew before, and with it some sparks of virtue began to kindle in his bosom. As he mused, the fire burnt within, and at last it made its way to his lips and vented itself. "Well," said he, "I have learnt two excellent lessons today, and I hope I shall never forgot them. There must be some vast and unknown pleasure in a virtuous love, beyond all the madness of wild and transient amours; otherwise the loss of the object could never have wrought such deep and unfeigned woe in a soul so firm and manly as that of Lucius. I begin now to believe what Milton sung, though I always read the lines before as mere poesy and fable.

> Hail wedded love, mysterious law, true source
> Of human offspring, solo propriety
> In Paradise, of all things common else:

By thee adulterous lust was driv'n from man
Among the bestial herds to range; by thee
Founded in reason, loyal, just, and pure,
Relations dear, and all the charities
Of father, son, and brother, first were known:
Perpetual fountain of domestic sweets.
Here love his golden shafts employs, here lights
His constant lamp, and waves his purple wings,
Reigns here and revels; not in the bought smile
Of harlots, loveless, joyless, unendear'd,
Casual amours, mixt dance, or wanton mask,
Or midnight ball," etc.

"Blessed poet, that could so happily unite love and virtue, and draw so beautiful a scene of real felicity, which till this day I always thought was merely romantic and visionary! Lucius has taught me to understand these lines, for he has felt them; and I think while I repeat them now I feel a strange new sensation. I am convinced the blind poet saw deeper into nature and truth than I could have imagined. There is, there is such a thing as a union of virtuous souls, where happiness is only found. I find some glimmerings of sacred light rising upon me, some unknown pantings within after such a partner and such a life.

"Nor is the other lesson which I have learnt at all inferior to this, but in truth it is of higher and more durable importance. I confess since I was nineteen years old I never thought virtue and religion had been good for any thing, but to tie up children from mischief, and to frighten fools: but now I find by the conduct of my friend Lucius, that as the sweetest and sincerest joys of life are derived from virtue, so the most distressing sorrows may find a just relief in religion and sincere piety. Hear me, thou Almighty Maker of my frame, pity and assist a returning wanderer, and O may thy hand stamp these lessons upon my soul in everlasting characters!" *Posthumous Works.*

BILLS OF EXCHANGE

When a rich merchant who dwells in a foreign land afar off, commits his treasure to the hands of a banker, it is to be drawn out in smaller sums by his servants or his friends here at home, as their necessities shall require; and he furnishes them with bills of exchange drawn upon his banker or treasurer, which are paid honorably to the person who offers the bill, according to the time when the words of the bill appoint the payment.

Is it not possible to draw a beautiful allegory hence to represent the conduct of the blessed God in his promises of grace, without debasing so divine a subject?

God the Father, the spring and fountain of all grace, dwells in regions of light and holiness inaccessible, too far off for us to converse with him or receive supplies from him in an immediate way; but he has sent the Son to dwell in human nature, and constituted him treasurer of all his blessings, that we might derive perpetual supplies from his hand: he has entrusted him with all the riches of grace and glory; he has laid up infinite stores of love, wisdom, strength, pardon, peace and consolation in the hands of his Son for this very purpose, to be drawn out thence as fast as the necessities of his saints require. "It pleased the Father that in him should all fullness dwell. He has received gifts for men."[1]

Now all the promises in the Bible, are so many bills of exchange drawn by God the Father in heaven, upon his Son Jesus Christ, and payable to every pious bearer; that is, to every one that comes to the mercy-seat and offers the promise for acceptance, and pleads it in a way of obedient faith and prayer. Jesus the high-treasurer of heaven, knows every letter of his Father's handwriting, and can never be imposed upon by a forged note; he will ever put due honor upon his Father's bills; he accepts them all, for "all the promises in him are yea, and in him amen." In him they are all sure "to the glory of the Father."[2] It is for the Father's honor that his bills never

1 Colossians 1:19; Psalm 68:18.
2 2 Corinthians 1:20.

fail of acceptance and payment.

If you apply to the blessed Jesus and offer him a bill of the largest sum, a promise of the biggest blessings, he will never say, "I have not so much of my Father's treasure in my hand. For he has received all things."[1] "The Father loveth the Son and hath given all things into his hand": and may I not venture to say, this whole treasure is made over to the saints, "All things are yours."[2] And they are parcelled out into bills of promise and notes under the Father's hand. So the whole treasure of a nation consists in credit and in promissory notes, more than in present sums of gold and silver.

Some of these divine bills are payable at sight, and we receive the sum as soon as we offer the bill; *viz*, those that must supply in our present wants; such as "call upon me in the day of trouble, and I will deliver thee, and thou shalt glorify me,"[3] and there have been many examples of such speedy payment. "In the day when I cried thou answered me; and strengthened me with strength in my soul."[4]

Some are only payable in general at a distant time, and that is left to the discretion of Christ the treasurer, *viz*. "As thy day is, so thy strength shall be,"[5] and we need never fear trusting him long, for this bank in the hands of Christ can never fail; "for in him dwelleth all the fullness of the Godhead bodily,"[6] we are told of "the unsearchable riches of Christ."[7]

Sometimes Christ may put us off with a general kind answer, or give us a note under his hand, payable at demand, in several parcels instead of a full payment all at once: thus he dealt with his dear friend and servant Paul, in 2 Corinthians 12:9. Doubtless Paul in his seeking the Lord thrice, for the removal of his thorn in the flesh, had pleaded several large promises of God, had offered those divine

1 John 3:35.
2 1 Corinthians 3:22.
3 Psalm 50:15.
4 Psalm 138:3.
5 Deuteronomy 33:25.
6 Colossians 2:9.
7 Ephesians 3:8.

bills to Christ for acceptance and payment; but instead of this our Lord gives him a note under his own hand which ran in this language, "My grace is sufficient for thee." And if we had but the faith which that blessed apostle had, we might live upon this hope; this would be as good as present payment: for if he delay to give the full sum, it is only because he sees we have not need of it at present: he knows our necessities better than we ourselves; he will not trust us with too much at once in our hands; but he pays us those bills when he sees the fittest time, and we have often found it so, and confessed his faithfulness.

At other times he pays us, but not in the same kind of mercy which is mentioned in the promise, yet in something more useful and valuable. If the promise mentions a temporal blessing, he may give us a spiritual one; if it express ease, he may give patience; and thus his Father's bills are always honored, and we have no reason to complain. So the banker may discharge a bill of a hundred pound not with money, but with such goods and merchandise as may yield us two hundred, and we gladly confess the bill is well paid.

Some of these promises, these bills of heavenly treasure, are not made payable till the hour of our death, as "Blessed are those servants whom when the Lord comes he shall find watching,"[1] etc. "He that endureth to the end the same shall be saved."[2] "Be thou faithful to the death, and I will give thee a crown of life."[3]

Others are not due till the day of the resurrection; as, "Them who sleep in Jesus will God bring with him."[4] "I will redeem them from death."[5] "When Christ who is our life shall appear, then shall ye also appear with him in glory."[6] "He shall change our vile body, that it may be fashioned like unto his glorious body."[7] "And when

1 Luke 12:37.
2 Matthew 24:13.
3 Revelation 2:10.
4 1 Thessalonians 4:14.
5 Hosea 13:14.
6 Colossians 3:4.
7 Philippians 3:20, 21.

the chief Shepherd shall appear, ye shall receive a crown of glory that fadeth not away."[1]

Now when the great day shall come, in which our Lord Jesus Christ shall give up his mediatorial kingdom to the Father, and render an account of all his stewardship, how fair will his books appear! How just a balance will stand at the foot of all his accounts! Then shall he show in what manner he has fulfilled the promises to the saints, and present to the Father all the bills that he has received and discharged; while all the saints shall with one voice attest it, to the honor of the high treasurer of heaven, that he has not failed in payment even to the smallest farthing. *Posthumous Works.*

---

1 1 Peter 5:1, 4.

POETRY

DIVINE JUDGMENTS

I.

Not from the dust my sorrows spring,
   Nor drop my comforts from the lower skies:
   Let all the baneful planets shed
   Their mingled curses on my head.
How vain their curses, if th' Eternal King
Look thro' the clouds and bless me with his eyes.
   Creatures, with all their boasted sway,
   Are but his slaves, and must obey;
   They wait their orders from above,
And execute his word, the vengeance, or the love.

II.

   'Tis by a warrant from his hand
   The gentler gales are bound to sleep:
The North wind blusters, and assumes command:
   Over the desert and the deep;
   Old Boreas with his freezing pow'rs
Turns the earth iron, makes the ocean glass,
Arrests the dancing riv'lets as they pass,
   And chains them moveless to their shores:
The grazing ox lows to the gelid skies,
Walks o'er the marble meads with withering eyes,
Walks o'er the solid lakes, snuffs up the wind, and dies.

III.

   Fly to the polar world, my song,
And mourn the pilgrims there, (a wretched throng!)
   Seized and bound in rigid chains,
A troop of statues on the Russian plains,
And life stands frozen in the purple veins.

Atheist, forbear, no more blaspheme:
God has a thousand terrors in his name,
   A thousand armies at command,
   Waiting the signal of his hand,
And magazines of frost, and magazines of flame.
   Dress thee in steel to meet his wrath;
   His sharp artillery from the north
Shall pierce thee to the soul, and shake thy mortal frame.
   Sublime on winter's rugged wings
   He rides in arms along the sky,
And scatters fate on swains and kings,
   And flocks and herds, and nations die;
   While impious lips, profanely bold,
Grow pale, and, quivering at his dreadful cold,
   Give their own blasphemies the lie.

IV.

   The mischiefs that infest the earth,
When the hot dog-star fires the realms on high,
   Drought, and disease, and cruel dearth,
Are but the flashes of a wrathful eye
   From the incens'd divinity.
   In vain our parching palates thirst,
For vital food in vain we cry,
     And pant for vital breath;
   The verdant fields are burnt to dust,
   The sun has drunk the channels dry,
     And all the air is death.
   Ye scourges of our Maker's rod,
'Tis at his dread command, at his imperial nod,
   You deal your various plagues abroad.

V.

Hail, whirlwinds, hurricanes, and floods,
   That all the leafy standards strip,

And bear down with a mighty sweep
The riches of the fields, and honors of the woods;
   Storms, that ravage o'er the deep,
   And bury millions in the waves;
   Earthquakes, that in midnight sleep
Turn cities into heaps, and make our beds our graves;
   While you dispense your mortal harms,
'Tis the Creator's voice that sounds your loud alarms,
When guilt with louder cries provokes a God to arms.

VI.

O for a message from above,
   To bear my spirits up!
Some pledge of my Creator's love,
To calm my terrors and support my hope!
   Let waves and thunders mix and roar,
Be thou my God, and the whole world is mine:
     While thou art Sovereign I'm secure;
   I shall be rich till thou art poor;
For all I fear, and all I wish, heav'n, earth, and hell, are thine.

THE UNIVERSAL HALLELUJAH
PSALM 148 PARAPHRASED

I.

Praise ye the Lord with joyful tongue,
   Ye powers that guard his throne;
Jesus, the man, shall lead the song,
   The God inspire the tune.

II.

Gabriel, and all th' immortal choir
   That fill the realms above,
Sing; for he form'd you of his fire,
   And feeds you with his love.

III.

Shine to his praise, ye crystal skies,
    The floor of his abode,
Or veil your little twinkling eyes,
    Before a brighter God.

IV.

Thou restless globe of golden light,
    Whose beams create our days,
Join with the silver queen of night,
    To own your borrowed rays.

V.

Blush and refund the honors paid
    To your inferior names;
Tell the blind world your orbs are fed
    By his o'erflowing flames.

VI.

Winds, ye shall bear his name aloud
    Through the ethereal blue,
For when his chariot is a cloud,
    He makes his wheels of you.

VII.

Thunder, and hail, and fires, and storms,
    The troops of his command,
Appear in all your dreadful forms
    And speak his awful hand.

VIII.

Shout to the Lord, ye surging seas,
    In your eternal roar;
Let wave to wave resound his praise,
    And shore reply to shore.

IX.

While monsters sporting on the flood,
    In scaly silver shine,
Speak terribly their maker God,
    And lash the foaming brine.

X.

But gentler things shall tune his name,
    To softer notes than these;
Young zephyrs breathing o'er the stream,
    Or whispering through the trees.

XI.

Wave your tall heads, ye lofty pines,
    To him that bids ye grow;
Sweet clusters bend the fruitful vines,
    On every thankful bough.

XII.

Let the shrill birds his honor raise,
    And climb the morning sky,
While groveling beasts attempt his praise
    In hoarser harmony.

XIII.

Thus while the meaner creatures sing,
    Ye mortals take the sound,
Echo the glories of your king
    Through all the nations round.

XIV.

Th' eternal name must fly abroad
    From Britain to Japan;
And the whole race shall bow to God,
    That owns the name of man.

THE DAY OF JUDGMENT
AN ODE
ATTEMPTED IN ENGLISH SAPPHIC

I.

When the fierce north wind, with his airy forces,
Rears up the Baltic to a foaming fury;
And the red lightning, with a storm of hail comes
      Rushing amain down,

II.

How the poor sailors stand amaz'd and tremble!
While the hoarse thunder, like a bloody trumpet,
Roars a loud onset to the gaping waters,
      Quick to devour them.

III.

Such shall the noise be, and the wild disorder,
(If things eternal may be like these earthly)
Such the dire terror, when the great archangel
      Shakes the creation;

IV.

Tears the strong pillars of the vault of heaven;
Breaks up old marble, the repose of princes;
See the graves open, and the bones arising,
      Flames all around them.

V.

Hark, the shrill outcries of the guilty wretches!
Lively bright horror, and amazing anguish,
Stare through their eye-lids, while the living worm lies
      Gnawing within them.

VI.

Thoughts, like old vultures, prey upon their heart strings,
And the smart twinges, when their eye beholds the

Lofty Judge frowning, and a flood of vengeance
    Rolling before him.

VII.

Hopeless immortals! how they scream and shiver,
While devils push them to the pit wide-yawning
Hideous and gloomy to receive them headlong
    Down to the center.

VIII.

Stop here, my fancy: (all away, ye horrid,
Doleful ideas,) come, arise to Jesus:
How he sits God-like! and the saints around him
    Thron'd, yet adoring!

IX.

O may I sit there when he comes triumphant,
Dooming the nations! then ascend to glory,
While our hosannas all along the passage
    Shout the Redeemer.

FIRE, AIR, EARTH, AND SEA, PRAISE YE THE LORD

I.

Earth, thou great footstool of our God
Who reigns on high; thou fruitful source
Of all our raiment, life, and food;
Our house, our parent, and our nurse;
    Mighty stage of mortal scenes,
    Drest with strong and gay machines,
    Hung with golden lamps around;
    (And flow'ry carpets spread the ground)
    Thou bulky globe, prodigious mass,
That hangs unpillar'd in an empty space!

While thy unwieldy weight rests on the feeble air,
Bless that Almighty word that fix'd and holds thee there.

II.

    Fire, thou swift herald of his face,
    Whose glorious rage, at his command,
    Levels a palace with the sand,
Blending the lofty spires in ruin with the base;
    Ye heav'nly flames that singe the air,
    Artillery of a jealous God,
Bright arrows that his sounding quivers bear
    To scatter deaths abroad;
Lightnings, adore the sovereign arm that flings
His vengeance, and your fires, upon the heads of kings.

III.

    Thou vital element, the air,
    Whose boundless magazines of breath
    Our fainting flame of life repair,
And save the bubble man from the cold arms of death;
And ye, whose vital moisture yields
    Life's purple stream, a fresh supply;
Sweet waters wand'ring thro' the flow'ry fields,
    Or dropping from the sky;
Confess the pow'r whose all-sufficient name
Nor needs our aid to build, or to support our frame.

IV.

    Now the rude air, with noisy force,
    Beats up and swells the angry sea,
    They join to make our lives a prey,
    And sweep the sailor's hopes away,
Vain hopes, to reach their kindred on the shores!
    Lo, the wild seas and surging waves
    Gape hideous in a thousand graves:

Be still, ye floods, and know your bounds of sand,
    Ye storms, adorn your Master's hand;
The winds are in his fist, the waves at his command.

V.

From the eternal emptiness
His fruitful word by secret springs
Drew the whole harmony of things
That form this noble universe:
Old nothing knew his pow'rful hand,
Scarce had he spoke his full command,
Fire, air, and earth, and sea, heard the creating call,
And leap'd from empty nothing to this beauteous all;
    And still they dance, and still obey
    The orders they receiv'd the great creation-day.

LAUNCHING INTO ETERNITY

It was a brave attempt! adventurous he,
Who in the first ship broke the unknown sea;
And leaving his dear native shores behind,
Trusted his life to the licentious wind.
I see the surging brine: the tempest raves:
He on a pine plank rides across the waves,
Exulting on the edge of thousand gaping graves:
He steers the winged boat, and shifts the sails,
Conquers the flood, and manages the gales.

    Such is the soul that leaves this mortal land
Fearless when the great Master gives command.
Death is the storm: she smiles to hear it roar,
And bids the tempest waft her from the shore:
Then with a skilful helm she sweeps the seas,
And manages the raging storm with ease;
("Her faith can govern death") she spreads her wings

Wide to the wind, and as she sails she sings,
And loses by degrees the sight of mortal things,
As the shores lessen, so her joys arise,
The waves roll gentler, and the tempest dies,
Now vast eternity fills all her sight,
She floats on the broad deep with infinite delight,
The seas forever calm, the skies for ever bright.

CONVERSE WITH CHRIST

I.
I'm tir'd with visits, modes, and forms,
And flatt'ries made to fellow worms;
    Their conversation cloys:
  Their vain amours and empty stuff:
  But I can ne'er enjoy enough
Of thy best company, my Lord, thou life of all my joys.

II.
  When he begins to tell his love,
  Through every vein my passions move,
    The captives of his tongue:
  In midnight shales, on frosty ground,
  I could attend the pleasing sound,
Nor should I feel December's cold, nor think the darkness long.

III.
  There while I hear my Saviour God
  Count o'er the sins (a heavy load!)
    He bore upon the tree,
  Inward I blush with secret shame,
  And weep, and love, and bless the name
That knew nor guilt nor grief his own, but bare *it all* for me.

IV.
  Next he describes the thorns he wore,

And talks his bloody passion o'er,
   'Till I am drown'd in tears:
Yet with the sympathetic smart
There's a strange joy beats round my heart;
The cursed tree has blessings in't, my sweetest balm it bears.

V.

I hear the glorious sufferer tell
How on his cross he vanquish'd hell,
   And all the pow'rs beneath:
Transported and inspir'd, my tongue
Attempts his triumphs in a song;
"How has the serpent lost his sting, and where's thy victory, death?"

VI.

But when he shows his hands and heart,
With those dear prints of dying smart,
   He sets my soul on fire:
Not the beloved John could rest
With more delight upon that breast,
Nor Thomas pry into those wounds with more intense desire.

VII.

Kindly he opens me his ear,
And bids me pour my sorrows there,
   And tell him all my pains:
Thus while I ease my burden'd heart,
In every woe he bears a part,
His arms embrace me, and his hand my drooping head sustains.

VIII.

Fly from my thoughts, all human things,
And sporting swains, and fighting kings,
   And tales of wanton love:
My soul disdains that little snare,

The tangles of Amira's hair;
Thine arms, my God, are sweeter bands, nor can my heart remove.

BREATHING TOWARD THE HEAVENLY COUNTRY
CASIMIRE, BOOK I. ODE 19. IMITATED.
Urit me Patriæ Decor, etc.

The beauty of my native land
Immortal love inspires;
I burn, I burn with strong desires,
And sigh, and wait the high command.
There glides the moon her shining way,
And shoots my heart through with a silver ray.
    Upward my heart aspires;
A thousand lamps of golden light
Hung high in vaulted azure charm my sight,
And wink and beckon with their amorous fires,
O ye fair glories of my heav'nly home,
    Bright sentinels who guard my Father' court,
    Where all the happy minds resort,
    When will my Father's chariot come?
Must ye for ever walk the ethereal round,
    For ever see the mourner lie
        An exile of the sky,
        A prisoner of the ground?
Descend some shining servant from on high,
    Build me a hasty tomb:
    A grassy turf will raise my head;
    The neighboring lilies dress my bed,
        And shed a sweet perfume.
Here I put off the chains of death
    My soul too long has worn;
    Friends, I forbid one groaning breath,
        Or tear to wet my urn;

Raphael, behold me all undrest,
Here gently lay this flesh to rest:
Then mount and lead the path unknown,
Swift I pursue thee, flaming guide, on pinions of my own.

FALSE GREATNESS

I.

Mylo, forbear to call him blest
That only boasts a large estate;
Should all the treasures of the west
Meet, and conspire to make him great.
I know thy better thoughts, I know
Thy reason can't descend so low.
Let a broad stream with golden sands
  Through all his meadows roll,
He's but a wretch, with all his lands,
  That wears a narrow soul.

II.

He swells amidst his wealthy store,
And proudly poising what he weighs,
In his own scale he fondly lays
  Huge heaps of shining ore.
He spreads the balance wide to hold
  His manors and his farms,
And cheats the beam with loads of gold
  He hugs between his arms.
So might the plough-boy climb a tree,
  When Crœsus mounts his throne,
And both stand up, and smile to see
  How long their shadow's grown.
Alas! how vain their fancies be,
  To think their shapes their own!

III.

Thus mingled still with wealth and state,
Crœsus himself can never know;
His true dimensions and his weight
Are far inferior to their show.
Were I so tall to reach the pole,
Or grasp the ocean with my span,
I must be measur'd by my soul:
The mind's the standard of the man.

TRUE MONARCHY
1701

The rising year beheld th' imperious Gaul
Stretch his dominion, while a hundred towns
Crouch'd to the victor: but a steady soul
Stands firm on its own base, and reigns as wide,
As absolute; and sways ten thousand slaves,
Lusts and wild fancies with a sovereign hand.

    We are a little kingdom; but the man
That chains his rebel will to reason's throne,
Forms it a large one, while his royal mind
Makes heaven its counsel, from the rolls above
Draws his own statutes, and with joy obeys.

    'Tis not a troop of well-appointed guards
Create a monarch, nor a purple robe
Dy'd in the people's blood; not all the crowns
Or dazzling tiaras that bend about the head,
Tho' gilt with sunbeams and set round with stars.
A monarch he that conquers all his fears,
And treads upon them; when he stands alone,
Makes his own camp, four guardian virtues wait
His nightly slumbers, and secure his dreams.

Now dawns the light; he ranges all his thoughts
In square battalions, bold to meet th' attacks
Of time and chance, himself a num'rous host,
All eye, all ear, all wakeful as the day,
Firm as a rock, and moveless as the center.

   In vain the harlot pleasure spreads her charms,
To lull his thoughts in luxury's fair lap,
To sensual ease, (the bane of little kings,
Monarchs whose waxen images of souls
Are moulded into softness) still his mind
Wears its own shape, nor can the heavenly form
Stoop to be model'd by the wild decrees
Of the mad vulgar, that unthinking herd.

   He lives above the crowd, nor hears the noise
Of wars and triumphs, nor regards the shouts
Of popular applause, that empty sound;
Nor feels the flying arrows of reproach,
Or spite or envy. In himself secure,
Wisdom his tow'r, and conscience is his shield,
His peace all inward, and his joys his own.

   Now my ambition swells, my wishes soar,
This be my kingdom: sit above the globe,
My rising soul, and dress thyself around,
And shine in virtue's armor; climb the height
Of wisdom's lofty castle, there reside,
Safe from the smiling and the frowning world.

   Yet once a day drop down a gentle look
On the great mole-hill, and, with pitying eye,
Survey the busy emmets round the heap,
Crowding and bustling in a thousand forms
Of strife and toil to purchase wealth and fame,

A bubble or a dust: then call thy thoughts
Up to thyself to feed on joys unknown,
Rich without gold, and great without renown.

FEW HAPPY MATCHES

AUGUST, 1701

I.

Say, mighty love, and teach my song,
To whom thy sweetest joys belong,
   And who the happy pairs
Whose yielding hearts, and joining hands,
Find blessings twisted with their bands,
   To soften all their cares.

II.

Not the wild herd of nymphs and swains
That thoughtless fly into the chains,
   As custom leads the way:
If there be bliss without design,
Ivies and oaks may grow and twine,
   And be as blest as they.

III.

Not sordid souls of earthly mold,
Who drawn by kindred charms of gold,
   To dull embraces move:
So two rich mountains of Peru
May rush to wealthy marriage too,
   And make a world of love.

IV.

Not the mad tribe that hell inspires
With wanton flames; those raging fires
   The purer bliss destroy:
On Ætna's top let furies wed,

And sheets of lightning dress the bed,
    T' improve the burning joy.

V.

Not the dull pairs, whose marble forms
None of the melting passions warms,
    Can mingle hearts and hands:
Logs of green wood that quench the coals
Are married just like stoic souls,
    With osiers for their bands.

VI.

Not minds of melancholy strain,
Still silent, or that still complain,
    Can the dear bondage bless:
As well may heavenly concerts spring
From two old lutes with ne'er a string,
    Or none beside the bass.

VII.

Nor can the soft enchantments hold
Two jarring souls of angry mold,
    The rugged and the keen:
Samson's young foxes might as well
In bands of cheerful wedlock dwell,
    With firebrands tied between.

VIII.

Nor let the cruel fetters bind
A gentle to a savage mind,
    For love abhors the sight:
Loose the fierce tiger from the deer,
For native rage and native fear
    Rise and forbid delight.

IX.

Two kindest souls alone must meet,
'Tis friendship makes the bondage sweet,
   And feeds their mutual loves:
Bright Venus on her rolling throne
Is drawn by gentlest birds alone,
   And Cupids yoke the doves.[1]

---

1 These poems are selected from *Horæ Lyricæ: or Poems Chiefly of the Lyric Kind*.

www.ingramcontent.com/pod-product-compliance
Lightning Source LLC
Chambersburg PA
CBHW070836100426
42813CB00003B/637